Classical Greek Art

Classical Greek Art

From the Age of Phidias
to the Age of Praxiteles

by
Charles Siegel

Omo Press

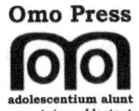

adolescentium alunt
senectutem oblectant

ISBN: 978-1-941667-30-9

Contents

Part 1
Background

Chapter 1
The Goal of this Book

Educated people know at least a bit about artists of Renaissance Italy and their works. Leonardo da Vinci painted the Mona Lisa and was not only a great artist but also an inventor. Michelangelo lay on his back to paint the Sistine ceiling. We appreciate their work all the more, because we know something about their lives.

Yet most people do not know the artists of classical Greece, even though they do know some of their works. The sculptures decorating the Parthenon are as important to the history of western art as the Mona Lisa or the Sistine ceiling. Yet few people know that Phidias and his workshop created these sculptures. Phidias was also the supervisor of all the construction on the Acropolis. His work was as important as Leonardo's and Michelangelo's, but few people know his name.

The Evidence

In part, the problem is that we know relatively little about the lives of the classical artists, because ancient Greece and Rome were aristocratic societies that looked down on anyone who performed manual labor. Plutarch explained why he did not write about artists by saying "Labour with one's own hands on lowly tasks gives witness ... to one's own indifference to higher things. No generous youth, from seeing the [statue of] Zeus at Pisa [Olympia], or the Hera at Argos, longs to be Phidias or Polyclitus…. For it does not of necessity follow that, if the work delights you with its grace, the one who wrought it is worthy of your esteem.[1]

Because most ancient writers considered these great artists to be manual laborers and beneath their notice, we have to reconstruct their history from scanty evidence.

One type of evidence is the writing that we have about the artists and their works, and there are two ancient books that discuss them in some detail. In the second century AD, the Greek geographer and traveler Pausanias wrote a long book named *Description of Greece*, which includes descriptions of many works of art and of their locations. In the first century AD, the Roman author Pliny the Elder wrote a book named *Natural History*, meant to be an encyclopedia of the knowledge of his time, and his sections on marble and metallurgy include long digression about marble and bronze statues and the artists who created them. Pliny gave dates for artists he mentioned, but unfortunately, he generally dated each of them to only one Olympiad—that is, to one four-year period—though their careers obviously lasted much longer than that. In addition to these two books, many other ancient authors also refer to artists briefly, but sometimes the accounts are contradictory; for example, we will see that there are two conflicting accounts of the death of Phidias.

The second type of evidence is, of course, the works of art themselves. Some original works survive, though generally in damaged form. Later copies of many works survive: the Greek originals were usually bronze, but Roman aristocrats loved having marble statues on their estates, so the copies are usually marble. and they are not always perfectly accurate. In addition, there are some pictures of ancient statues on coins, issued by cities that were proud to have these works of art.

Most histories of classical art include artists whose works we know based only on descriptions. This comprehensive approach has value as history, but it gets in the way of understanding the art by cluttering up the books with descriptions of works and artists who were considered important in ancient times but whom we cannot appreciate today because we cannot see their works.

Likewise, most histories include works whose artists we do not know or whose attribution is disputed. Again, this has value of history, but we can understand a work better if we know something about the artist and his other works, and it is a distraction to clutter up the history with discussions of controversies about the attribution of works.

This book only includes artists whose work survives — usually in the form of copies—and only works whose artists we know. It also summarizes what we know about the artists' lives, since we can appreciate the works better if we know something about the people who created them. It includes all the artists of the classical period whose works survive and sometimes (if it helps to understand their careers) a bit about their other works that exist only through descriptions.

The best way to understand classical art and to see how it reflected the history of its times is to look at individual artists chronologically so we can compare the artists and their works.

A Note About Spelling

Ancient Greek art was the beginning of a living tradition of classical and neoclassical art that extended through Roman times, through the Renaissance, and into the early twentieth century. This living tradition generally referred to the ancient Greek artists by using Latinized version of their names. In the course of the twentieth century, though, modern artists stopped being inspired by these classical artists so they became part of history rather than of a living tradition, it became common to use names based more closely on the original Greek but written in our alphabet, treating the artists as ancient history rather than as part of a living tradition. For example, the artist whose Latinized name is Phidias and who was called Phidias through the nineteenth century now is often called Pheidias.

There are several common differences between the traditional Latinized spelling and the modern transliterated Greek spelling of names. The regular differences, which we see over and over again, are:

The *k* in transliterated Greek becomes a *c* in Latin.

The *ei* in transliterated Greek becomes an *i* in Latin.

The ending *os* in transliterated Greek becomes *us* in Latin.

The oi in transliterated Greek becomes oe in Latin.

The ai in transliterated Greek becomes ae in Latin.

For many names, there is no difference, because they do not include these letters.

For some names, these general rules are commonly broken. For example, Polykleitos is often Latinized as Polycletus instead of Polyclitus, and some modern authors spell it Polycleitus. Kritios was invariably Latinized as Critas instead of Critius, following a corrupt manuscript of Pliny,[2] which had an error that was probably introduced by a copyist thinking of the famous Critias who was a leader of Athens' government after the Peloponnesian War.

Because this book values classical art as a living tradition, it uses the Latinized spelling of people's names, and it applies the general rules consistently, so it calls these two artists Polyclitus and Critius. At the beginning of the chapters about the artists and when other names are first mentioned, this book also gives the transliterated Greek spelling in parentheses if the two are different. Readers who want more information about these artists should look up both the Latin and the transliterated Greek names.

This book also changes the spelling of names in quotation to the Latinized spelling.

Many works of art have Greek names, and this book uses the transliterated Greek spelling with the translation in parentheses, such as Doryphoros (Spear Carrier). Occasionally, works are so well known that their Greek names are often Latinized, such as Discobolus for Diskobolos (Discus Thrower), but for the sake of consistency, this book uses transliterated Greek spellings for the names of works of art.

Chapter 2
The Historical Context

This is a book about art, not history, but to understand the classical works of art, it is essential to understand their historical context, so we will begin with the briefest possible summary of the history of the times.

The Persian Invasion
(499 BC to 478 BC)

In the Persian War, a Greece that was divided into small city-states repelled an invasion by the most powerful empire of the time.

The Persian Empire under Cyrus the Great had conquered the Middle East, including the Greek settlements in Ionia (now part of Turkey). In 499 BC, a Greek general incited these settlements to revolt. In 494, the Persians had put down this revolt and vowed to punish Greece.

The first invasion of Greece was partly successful. In 492, the Persians invaded and conquered parts of Greece, but in 490, Athens stopped the Persian forces at the Battle of Marathon.

The second invasion, led by the Persian emperor Xerxes began in 480. After the Athenians evacuated on ships rather than defending the city, the Persians tore down Athens' walls, started fires, and destroyed the city completely. But the Greek cities were united against them, and a Greek fleet destroyed much of the Persian fleet at the Battle of Salamis. The next year, the Greek armies decisively defeated the Persians at the Battle of Plataea, ending the Persian invasion.

In 478 BC, Greek cities formed an alliance under Athenian leadership, called the Delian League, because the Spartan general

Pausanias was suspected of conspiring with Xerxes, and they won all of Greece and Ionia back from the Persians. In 451 BC, they invaded Cyprus with little success, and the Persian wars ended when they withdrew.

The Golden Age
(478 - 431 BC)

When the Persian invasion ended, the golden age of Athens began—a half century of prosperity when there was an unprecedented flourishing of art and culture. After the Delian League began winning the series of battles that drove the Persians out of Greece and Ionia, Athenians began to rebuilt their devastated city.

Pericles (Perikles), general and statesman, led Athens from about 461 to 429 BC. Though slavery was common and women were excluded from public life, male citizens governed Athens as a radical democracy, where all male citizens were allowed to attend the Assembly, which passed laws, and where most officials were chosen by lot. Ten generals were elected for one-year terms, one of the very few elected offices. Pericles was reelected year after year and became the most influential person in government.

During the Golden age, the Delian League gradually changed from an alliance of free cities into something more like an Athenian empire. In 454 BC, Pericles moved the Delian League treasury from Delos to Athens and used it to finance massive rebuilding of the Acropolis, claiming that Athens "owed no account of their moneys to the allies provided it carried on the war for them and kept off the Barbarians."[3] This has been called the most artistically fruitful embezzlement in history, since funds taken from the Delian League financed the Parthenon and other great architecture and art on the Acropolis.

The Peloponnesian War
(431-404 BC)

Sparta was Athens' main rival, and it responded to increased Athenian power by forming the Peloponnesian League, an alliance of cities on the Peloponnese, the southern part of Greece, connected to the rest of Greece by a narrow isthmus.

In 431 BC, war broke out between Athens's Delian League and Sparta's Peloponnesian League. Sparta repeatedly invaded Attica (the peninsula where Athens is located), while Athens used its naval supremacy to raid the coast of the Peloponnese. In 430-426 BC, there was a series of plagues in Athens, spread in part because it was overcrowded with people who had fled into the city as the enemy ravaged the surrounding countryside. These plagues killed Pericles and about 100,000 people, and they undermined morality and religion.

In 421 BC, there was a temporary and imperfect truce called the Peace of Nicias, which was undermined by fighting in the Peloponnese and formally abandoned in 414 BC. In 415 BC, Athens sent a large force to attack Syracuse, a Greek colony in Sicily, but this force was totally destroyed. Sparta, aided by the Persians, supported rebellions of Athens' subject states in Ionia and the Aegean Sea. In 405 BC, Sparta destroyed Athens' navy in the Battle of Aegospotami, effectively ending the war. In 404 BC, Athens formally surrendered.

The war caused massive destruction throughout Greece. Athens never recovered the prosperity of its golden age.

After the Peloponnesian War (404-323 BC)

The political situation in Athens and Greece was chaotic after the Peloponnesian War.

In 404 BC, after Athens' defeat, thirty aristocrats with Spartan support took over Athens' government. They were known as the "thirty tyrants." For about eight months, they presided over a reign of terror, killing about 5% of Athens' population and exiling many others to protect their own power. A group of exiles, led by the moderate democrat Thrasybulus, attacked and defeated the thirty. Sparta sent a force to attack the democrats, but instead negotiated with them and allowed a moderate democracy to be restored— perhaps because the Spartans themselves realized that the thirty tyrants had been a bloody failure.

There were minor wars among cities during this period. Most important, in 371 BC, Thebes defeated Sparta and became the dominant city-state in Greece for a time. Persia took advantage of these conflicts to keep Greece weak: its strategy in each war was to oppose the stronger city, so no city could become the leader of Greece and threaten Persia.

In 338 BC, King Phillip II of Macedon defeated a combined Theban and Athenian army, and in 337, he formed the League of Corinth, which made him the ruler of a federated Greece. But he was not ruler for long: in 336 BC, he was assassinated and was succeeded by his son, who came to be known as Alexander the Great. Alexander conquered most of the known world using the new military formation that his father had invented, the Macedonian Phalanx. In 323 BC, Alexander died in Babylon at the age of 32.

Historians generally consider Alexander's death in 323 BC to be the end of the classical period and beginning of the Hellenistic period, when Greek culture fused with the cultures of the nations he had conquered. Alexander's empire split into several empires, which were dominated by Greeks politically and culturally. But many of their important cultural centers were outside of Greece— for example, in Alexandria, Egypt, which Alexander had founded and named after himself, Most important the Hellenistic Greeks lived in empires rather than the self-governing city-states that classical Greece believed were a necessary part of the good life.

The Flowering of Culture

There was an unprecedented flowering of culture in Athens and Greece during the classical period—beginning in the golden age and continuing through the period after the Peloponnesian War.

Aeschylus invented the drama during the golden age: he added a second actor to the traditional recitation by one actor and a chorus. His successors Sophocles and Euripides continued writing great tragedies during and after the Peloponnesian War.

Herodotus and Thucydides invented the modern writing of history, the former writing about the Persian Wars and the latter about the Peloponnesian War.

Hippocrates revolutionized medicine during the golden age.

Plato and Aristotle created the most important works of ancient philosophy after the Peloponnesian war.

As we will see, classical art also flowered during this entire period: Phidias and his contemporaries flourished during the golden age, and Praxiteles and his contemporaries after the Peloponnesian war.

Though most of this flowering of culture was centered in Athens, we will see that there was also an important group of artists in Argos, which is in the Peloponnese but was never an ally of Sparta and was a democracy during most of the classical period. Thus, there were two important schools of art in classical times, the Attic school centered in Athens (capital of Attica) and the Argive school centered in Argos.

Chapter 3
Before Classical Art

This book focuses on the classical Greek sculptors, who have had an immense influence on Western art, but we will begin with a brief look at Greek sculpture before their time, because the contrast shows how great the accomplishment of the classical artists was.

Archaic Art

During the archaic period, from about 650 to 480 BC, Greek sculptors imitated Egyptian and Babylonian models, and their work was crude and unnatural. Two common types of sculpture in the archaic period were a standing nude young man (called a Kouros) and a standing clothed woman (called a Kore).

As we can see in the two Kouros statues of Cleobis (Kleobis) and Biton, from about 580 BC, archaic sculptures were stylized, stiff and conventional.

Cleobis and Biton were two brothers from Argos whose mother was a priestess of Hera. When her oxen could not be found, the brothers themselves pulled their mother in her cart six miles to the Temple as part of a ceremony she had to perform. She prayed to Hera to reward them, and Hera took their lives, giving them the reward of a good death. Solon listed the brothers as two of the three happiest people he knew of,[4] showing that the ancient Greeks felt very differently about this reward than we would,

The people of Argos dedicated these statues by Polymedes of Argos in Delphi to honor the brothers, showing that the Argive artistic tradition had deep roots. They were found in Delphi by archeologists in the nineteenth century. The names Cleobis and Biton are inscribed on their bases, but they are obviously icons meant to symbolize the brothers rather than attempts to show what

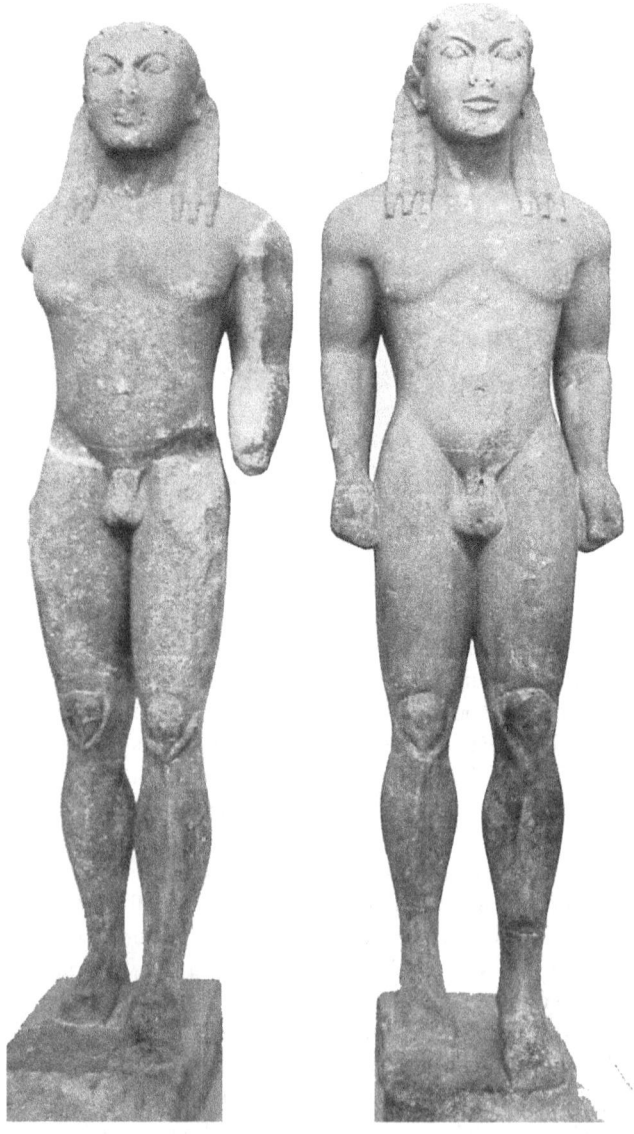

Figure 3-1: Cleobis and Biton, Kouroi of the Archaic period, Archeological
Museum of Delphi

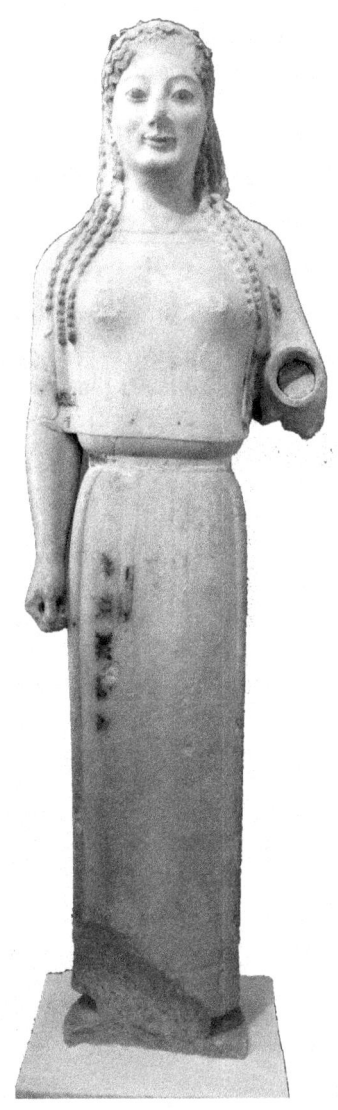

**Figure 3-2: Peplos Kore, Kore of the Archaic Period,
Acropolis Museum**

the brothers actually looked like. The faces and bodies are almost identical.

Likewise, the statue of Peplos Kore, so called because she wears a shawl called a peplos, is stiff and unnatural. This statue was found in three pieces in 1886 in an excavation of the Acropolis of Athens and dates to about 530 BC. We can see that there was essentially no artistic progress in the fifty years between the statues of Cleobis and Biton and the Peplos Kore.

Pre-Classical Art: Critius

The generation immediately before the earliest classical sculptors moved from the archaic towards the classical style. The most important sculptor of this time was Critius (Kritios), who worked after the end of the Persian invasion but before the beginning of the golden age.

Harmodius and Aristogiton

In 477-476 BC, shortly after Athens drove the Persians out of Greece, statues of the tyrannicides Harmodius (Harmodios) and Aristogiton (Aristogeiton) were set up on the Acropolis[5] to replace earlier statues of them by Antenor that the Persians had looted in 480 BC. These two tyranicides were killed after they assassinated the tyrant Hipparchus at the Panathenaic Festival of 514 BC, paving the way for Athenian democracy. These replacement statues were by Critius and Nesiotes, who was probably an assistant of Critius.[6] It is interesting to see that these statues were installed so soon after the Persian invasion was ended and that Athens commissioned these statues honoring democracy as some of the earliest to be restored.

There is a huge difference between the Kouros and Kore sculptures and these sculptures, with a much more naturalistic representation of anatomy and representation of individual features, but the style is still stiff and severe.

Ephebos (Boy)

Critius also did a statue that was found during excavations of the Acropolis in the nineteenth century, which is called Ephebos

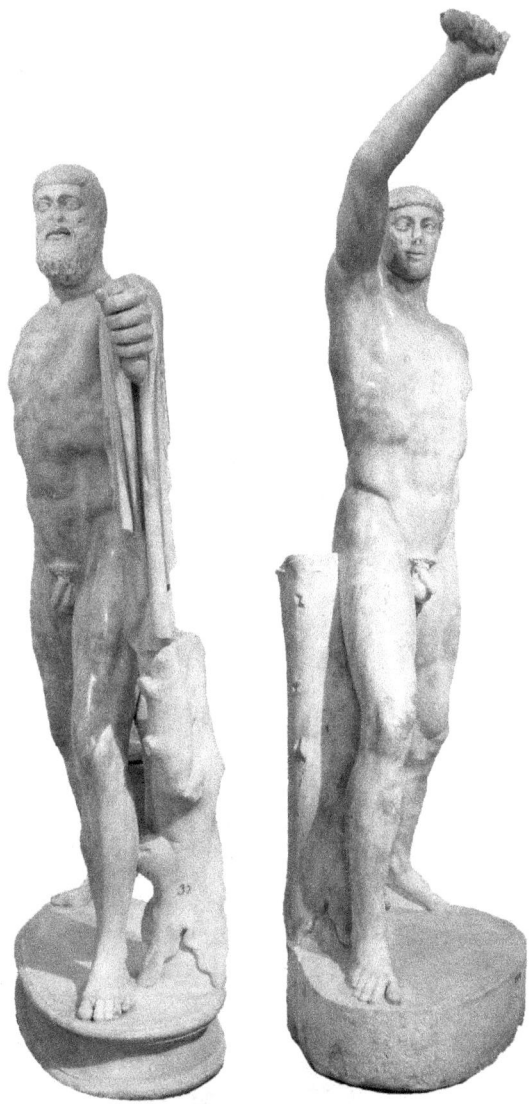

**Figure 3-3: Roman Copies of Harmodius and Aristogiton,
National Archeological Museum in Naples**

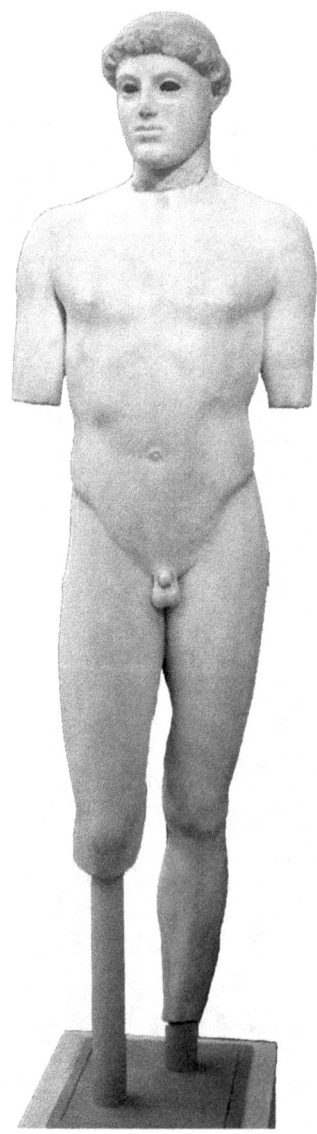

**Figure 3-4: Ephebos (Boy),
Acropolis Museum, Athens.**

(Boy). Here the musculature and the posture seems to be more natural than in the statues of the tyrannicides, anticipating the classical style of the next generation. But when we compare it with the classical statues that we will look at in the coming chapters, we can see that it is somewhere between the conventionalized style of the archaic age and the naturalism of the classical age.

Nevertheless, there was considerable progress during the fifty years between the Peplos Kore and works of Critius—a sharp contrast with the stagnation during the fifty years between Biton and Cleobis and Peplos Kore.

Contrapposto Posture

Critius' Ephebos is the earliest surviving example of the contrapposto posture, which was very important in the classical period (as we will see) and was revived during the renaissance—when it got the name "contrapposto," Italian for "counterpoise."

The figure rests its weight on one leg, so the shoulders are not directly above the hips, making it look more natural and creating a sense of poise and stability.

As we will see, the classical sculptors commonly used the contrapposto posture and carried it further than Critius did.

Part 2
The Age of Phidias

The first period of classical art began a couple of decades after the Persian War ended in 478 BC. It was generally agreed in ancient times that its three greatest artists were Phidias, Myron and Polyclitus, and we are lucky to have works by all three. Phidias and Myron were based in Athens, and Polyclitus was based in Argos.

Pliny dates Phidias to the 83rd Olympiad (448-444 BC). He dates both Myron and Polyclitus to the 90th Olympiad (420-416 BC), which is after Phidias death and during the Peloponnesian War. Of course, their careers all lasted far longer than four years and undoubtedly overlapped, but it is clear that Phidias was the earliest of the three, though some art historians say Myron and Polyclitus were earlier,[7] apparently just because Phidias' style seems more advanced.

Polyclitus specialized in stable figures standing in the contrapposto position. Myron specialized in dynamic figures caught in the midst of motion. Phidias did both, as well as doing huge cult statues.

There are also surviving sculptures by another contemporary of these three, Cresilas, who was trained in Argos and worked in Athens.

Chapter 4
Phidias

The ancients considered Phidias (Pheidias) to be the greatest sculptor of all time. We have more information about him than about other artists—but still not enough to let us reconstruct his career with certainty.

He was born in the 490s or 480s BC (estimates range from 500 to 480). His father's name was Charmides. There are a number of conflicting suggestions about who his teachers were, but in any case, their style was probably like the style of Critius, which we looked at in the previous chapter, part of the way to the classical style but not there yet.

Plutarch tells us that enemies of Pericles accused him of including a portrait of himself on the shield of Athena Parthenos in the Parthenon—"when he wrought the battle of the Amazons on the shield of the goddess, he carved out a figure that suggested himself as a bald old man lifting on high a stone with both hands"[8]—and also including a figure that suggested Pericles. A large part of a Roman copy of the shield has survived (see Figure 4-6), and it includes this picture of Phidias lifting an axe with both hands rather than the stone that Plutarch mentions, because either Plutarch or the Roman copy of the shield is not perfectly accurate.

It is likely that the figure on the shield actually is a portrait of Phidias as he looked late in his life, when he was working on the Athena Parthenos, but with an idealized body. Older people do not appear elsewhere in the art of the classical period, and the most probable reason that one appears here is that it is a self-portrait of Phidias.

Plutarch also tells us that Phidias was a friend of Pericles and that Pericles' enemies claimed that he "made assignations for Pericles with free-born women who would come ostensibly to see the works of art. The comic poets took up this story and bespattered Pericles with charges of abounding wantonness..."⁹ We can dismiss this accusation as a political slur, but it does show that the two were close friends.

Plutarch gives us the following account of his death. Enemies of Pericles convinced Phidias' assistant Menon to bring charges against him, and he accused Phidias of embezzlement, of stealing some of the gold that had been allocated to create the statue of Athena Parthenos in the Parthenon. But Pericles had suggested when the project began that Phidias should design the gold so it could be removed, so he answered the charges by weighing the gold to prove that none had been taken. Then Pericles' enemies accused Phidias of blasphemy for including pictures of himself and of Pericles on the shield of Athena, and he died in jail. The assembly gave Menon freedom from taxation as a reward.¹⁰

Another source says that Phidias was exiled by the enemies of Pericles, worked on the Olympian Zeus in Elis while he was in exile, and was executed by the Eleans after completing this statue for them. The appendix looks at how reliable these two accounts of Pericles death are.

This chapter arranges his works based on a plausible reconstruction of the order in which they were produced, assuming that he produced Olympian Zeus earlier in his career rather than as his final work after being exiled.

Regardless of whether Phidias died in jail or went into exile, Pericles decided he had to consolidate his power after his friend was convicted, and as a result, he reaffirmed trade sanctions against Megara, causing the Peloponnesian War.¹¹

Phidias' later projects were so large that he built workshops at Olympia and on the Acropolis where many artists worked on them. Some of these artists were famous in their own right in ancient times, such as his favorite disciples Agoracritus (Agorakritos) and Alcamenes (Alkamanes). It is not possible to attribute the individual decorative sculptures of the Parthenon to Phidias or to others in his workshop, but there is one work that we can attribute to Agoracritus, which is shown in Chapter 8 of this book.

This chapter includes early works by Phidias and later works by his workshop, which show Phidias' ideas about art, though we cannot be sure whether he worked on any of them himself.

The ancients most admired Phidias' huge chryselephantine (gold and ivory) works, the Zeus in Olympia, Elea, and the Athena Parthenos in Athens. In retrospect, we most admire the decorative marble sculptures of the Parthenon, because they began the classical tradition that produced the greatest art of the millennia that followed.

Notice that all his works are either civic art, monuments to prominent people, or religious art, which was also a form of civic art in the Greek city-states, which had state religions.

Anacreon

A copy of one of Phidias' early works has survived, which helps us to understand his artistic development. His bronze statue of the poet Anacreon on the Acropolis was probably created when Phidias was in his twenties. A Roman copy in marble was found in an ancient Roman villa near Lieti.

The figure stands in the contrapposto position that is common in classical works, resting his weight on one leg. The human figure is much more skillfully done than the works of the previous generation. Its rendering of the musculature is much more naturalistic than in Critius' Boy, and its face is much more individualized than the generic face of Critius' Boy. Though Anacreon lived before his time, Phidias clearly imagined him as an individual.

But the cloth draped around his shoulders is flat and stiff and does not look like actual drapery. The clumsy execution of the drapery is a sign that this is an early work, and we will see that there is much more naturalistic and dynamic representation of drapery later in his career. This relatively small early work was presumably done by Phidias himself, not by a large workshop.

Athena Lemnia

There is another surviving work that is probably from Phidias' early period, the Athena Lemnia.

Pausanius[12] wrote that Phidias created a bronze statue for

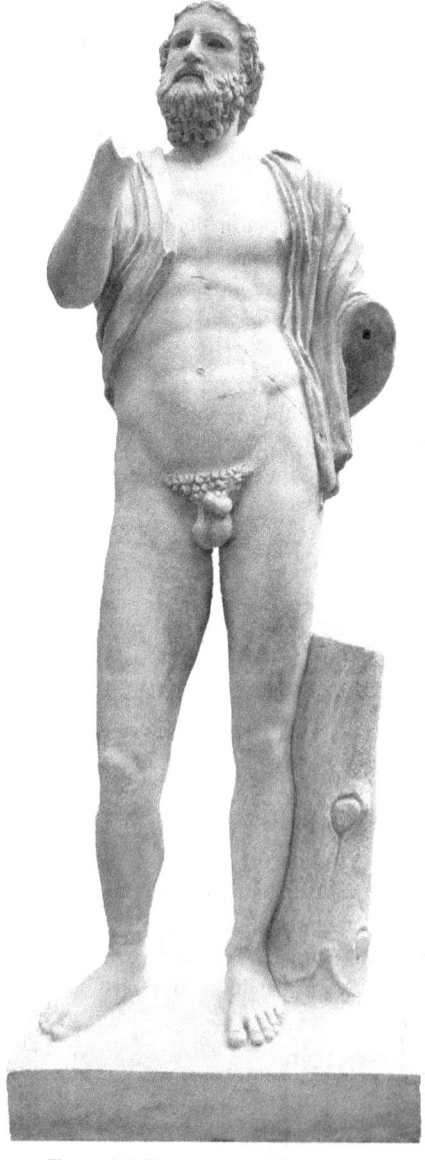

Figure 4-1: Roman copy of Anacreon,
Ny Carlsberg Glyptotek.

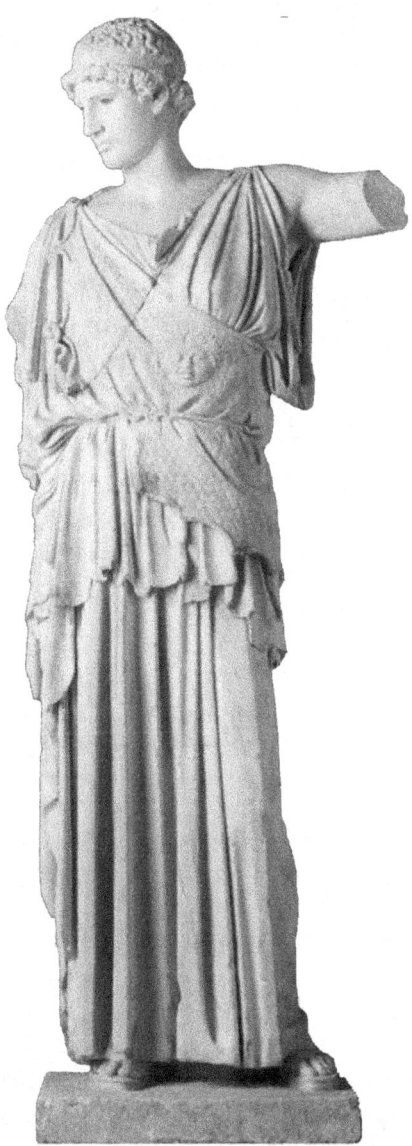

**Figure 4-2: Reconstructed Athena Lemnia,
Staatliche Kunstsammlungen Dresden**

Athenians living in Lemnia to dedicate on the Acropolis. In 1891, the German archeologist Adolf Furtwängler reconstructed this statue from Roman copies in marble. Two copies of the entire statue with their heads badly damaged survived, as did two copies of just the head.

Athena wears an aegis and gorgonian. There are two different versions of these typical attributes of Athena. Usually, the aegis is a shield and the gorgonian is a picture of a gorgon in archaic style that is in the center of the shield, as in Phidias' later Athena Parthenos. Sometimes, the aegis is an animal skin worn over ordinary clothing to provide extra protection, and the gorgonian is an amulet depicting the head of a gorgon in archaic style that is attached to the aegis, as in this version. In this statue, Athena probably also held a spear in her left hand.

Because it is a female statue, it is clothed, so we cannot compare the execution of the body to Phidias' Anacreon. The facial features are individualized, like Anacreon's. The drapery is skillfully done: it is not caught in action, flowing in the wind, like many of the marbles from the Parthenon, but it is naturalistic, not nearly as stiff and artificial as the drapery of Phidias' Anacreon.

Furtwängler dated the original by Phidias to 451-448. Because it is only 2 meters (just over 6 feet) high, it makes more sense to date it at least a bit earlier, before Phidias started getting commissions for much larger projects that required a large workshop to execute.

It is plausible that this statue was done before Phidias' time was taken up by larger projects and after the Anacreon, since the more naturalistic drapery shows that it was done by a more mature and more skilled Phidias

Monument to Miltiades

Pausanias tells us that Phidias did many of the statues in a group of bronze statues that Athenians dedicated at Delphi from their tithe of the Persian spoils, showing the Athenian general Miltiades surrounded by Athena, Apollo, and heroes of Athenian clans.[13]

A century ago, these statues were widely considered early works and probably Phidias' earliest major works.[14] More recently, some scholars have said they were late works, commissioned by

Miltiades son Cimon (Kimon) after he returned from exile. If we look at the historical background, it seems more plausible that they were early works.

Miltiades was the general whose troops won the Battle of Marathon in 490 BC, the first major victory of the Greeks in the Persian Wars. His son Cimon was a prominent general and statesman who became a hero after defeating the Persian fleet in the battle of Salamis (480 BC). In the 460s BC, Cimon became a leader of the aristocratic faction opposing the democratic reforms supported by Pericles, who was head of the democratic faction. Cimon advocated for peace with Sparta and cooperation with the

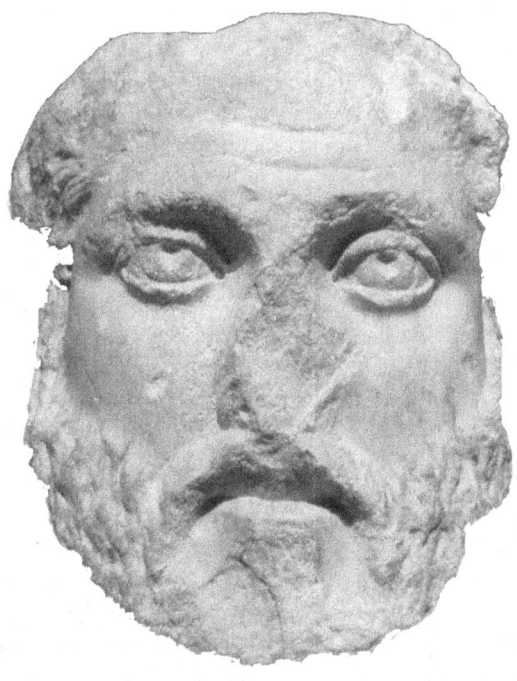

Figure 4-3: Face of Miltiades, Acropolis Museum

aristocrats who controlled that city. In 462 BC, he led a failed expedition to Sparta to help its aristocrats put down a rebellion by their slaves, the Helots. This loss harmed his reputation, and in 461 BC, he was ostracized. Ostracism was a vote of the Athenian assembly that exiled someone from the city for ten years but allowed him to keep his property. In about 451 BC, Cimon was called back to Athens to negotiate a peace treaty between Athens and Sparta, and in 449 BC, he died during a battle with the Persians in Cyprus.

It is not plausible that Phidias worked on this monument after Cimon returned from exile. By that time, Phidias was working on large projects on the Acropolis, and it is unlikely that he had time to take on a major project outside of Athens. By that time, also, Phidias was a friend of Pericles, and it is not likely that he would help a rival of Pericles advance his political career in this way. The idea that Cimon commissioned this monument also contradicts Pausanias' statement that it was paid for by the spoils of Marathon, though Pausanias is not always reliable about details like this. Thus, this is likely an earlier work commissioned by the city of Athens and one of Phidias' earliest works on a larger scale, with more than one statue.

All that survives from this monumental group is the face of Miltiades, found by archeologists at Delphi. It is noteworthy because it is clearly has an individual's features and reveals something of the individual's character, rather than being the generic face that we find on many sculptures of the time.

Olympian Zeus

Phidias' chryselephantine (gold and ivory) statue of Zeus at Olympia was his most admired work in ancient times and was considered one of the Seven Wonders of the World. Pliny called it a statue "which no one has ever equalled."[15] Pausanias tells us about a legend that shows how much the statue was admired by the bronze jar standing in fron of it: "when the image was quite finished Phidias prayed the god to show by a sign whether the work was to his liking. Immediately, runs the legend, a thunderbolt fell on that part of the floor where ... the bronze jar stood to cover the place."[16]

This statue was commissioned by the city-state of Elis for the new temple of Zeus that they were building at the city of Olympia, where the Olympic Games were held. It is often called the Olympic Zeus, using the adjective for the city's name. The statue was over 40 feet high, a huge project, and Phidias built a workshop for his team near the site, which was rediscovered by archeologists in 1954-1958.

Today, the statue survives only in descriptions and pictures in coins. Pausanias described it as follows:

The god sits on a throne, and he is made of gold and ivory. On his head lies a garland which is a copy of olive shoots. In his right hand he carries a Victory, which, like the statue, is of ivory and gold; she wears a ribbon and—on her head—a garland. In the left hand of the god is a scepter, ornamented with every kind of metal, and the bird sitting on the scepter is the eagle. The sandals also of the god are of gold, as is likewise his robe. On the robe are embroidered figures of animals and the flowers of the lily.[17]

Scholars who believe Phidias was exiled from Athens and that the Eleans executed him when this work was complete, obviously believe that it was his last work, so they give it a later date. Here, we are reconstructing his career based on the other version of his death, so we give it an earlier date, before he began work on the Parthenon. See the Appendix for more information about these accounts of his death.

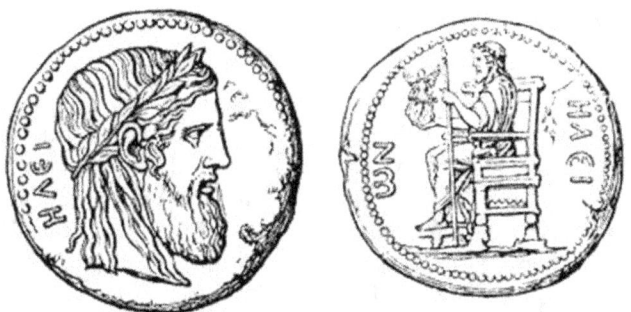

Figure 4-4: Phidias' Olympian Zeus shown on a coin from the district of Elis, where the statue was located

This work fits plausibly into Phidias' career at this earlier time. The work on the monument to Miltiades in Elis showed his ability to do larger, more complex projects. helping him to get bigger commissions.

Pausanias mentions a few works that could have continued to build his reputation to the point where he was given this huge commission to create Olympian Zeus. In Elis, he created chryselephantine Aphrodite Urania standing with one foot on a tortoise[18] and also a chryselephantine Athena with the image of a cock on her helmet.[19] In Platea, he built a statue of Athena that was made of gilded wood and had face, hands, and feet of marble, which was almost as large as the Athena Promachos on the Acropolis of Athens[20] (which we will look at next).

By including these projects, it is easy to imagine a plausible career path for Phidias. His early individual statues were so excellent that they earned him the commission to do the monument to Miltiades in Delphi. The success of this monument earned his commissions to do the two chryselephantine statues in Elea and the huge statue of Athena in Platea.[21] The success of these works built up his reputation to the point where he got the commission to do the huge chryselephantine Olympian Zeus, which made him the foremost artist and manager of teams of artists in Greece and earned him the commissions to supervise all the building on the Acropolis of Athens and to create his own monumental works there, beginning with the Athena Promachos.

Athena Promachos

Phidias' Athena Promachos was the largest outdoor figure on the Acropolis: the bronze statue itself was 25 or 30 feet high, and in combination with its pedestal, it was about 70 feet high. Pausanias called it "the bronze Athena" but in the fifth century AD it was moved to Constantinople, and after that time it was called Athena Promachos, which means "Athena the forward fighter."

It is known only from pictures on coins and descriptions, such as this one from the Byzantine historian Niketas:

The goddess wore an ankle-length garment tightly belted at the waist and over it an aegis, complete with gorgoneion. Her neck

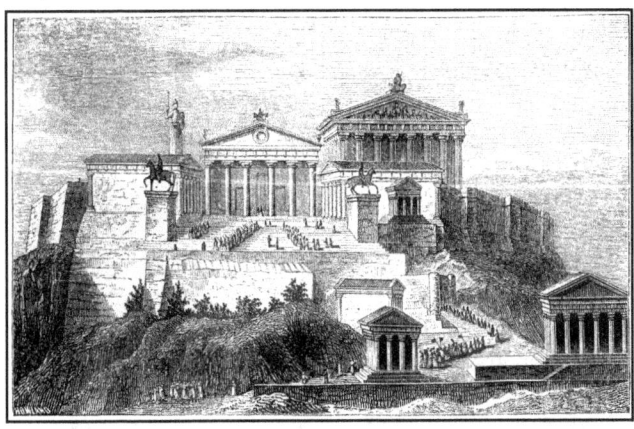

Figure 4-5: Late nineteenth century engraving showing how Athena Promachos (upper left) stood out in the skyline of the Acropolis

was uncovered. On her head she wore a helmet with a horse-hair crest and her hair could be seen escaping from beneath the helmet on to her forehead. At the back, the hair was plaited. Her left hand held the folds of her dress, while the right was outstretched towards the south.[22]

It was the most prominent landmark in Athens. According to Pausanias, the tip of Athena's helmet and the point of her spear were visible to ships from miles away.[23]

Pausanias says this statue was financed with the spoils from the Persian War, but this does not seem plausible. The shift to a much larger scale implies that the other buildings on the Acropolis were arranged around it and that there must have been a new infusion of money that started this new building boom, so it makes more sense that this statue was built after Pericles had taken the Delian treasury to fund massive projects on the Acropolis—or at least, after he had made Phidias supervisor of construction and Phidias began to lay out massive rebuilding of the Acropolis, including this statue and all the new buildings around it

The illustration is an imaginary nineteenth century visualization of Athena Promachos, showing how it rose above the Acropolis.

The Parthenon

Pericles made Phidias supervisor of all the building on the Acropolis and gave him the commission to create the sculptures for the Parthenon. As we have seen, the Acropolis had been destroyed by the Persians, and monuments began being rebuilt there after the Persian invasion ended, but the rebuilding accelerated dramatically when Pericles moved the treasury of the Delian League to Athens in 454 BC and began spending some of this money on the Acropolis.

In about 447 BC, Phidias and his assistants built a workshop on the Acropolis and he and his team of artists began work on these sculptures. Ictinus and Callicrates were architects of the Parthenon.[24] Phidias produced so many sculptures for the Parthenon that we need several subsections to describe them.

Athena Parthenos

The ancients considered the chryselephantine statue of Athena in the Parthenon to be its greatest sculpture. It was about 38 feet tall. Pausanius describes it as follows:

The statue itself is made of ivory and gold. On the middle of her helmet is placed a likeness of the Sphinx ... and on either side of the helmet are griffins in relief. ... The statue of Athena is upright, with a tunic reaching to the feet, and on her breast the head of Medusa is worked in ivory. She holds a statue of Victory about four cubits high, and in the other hand a spear; at her feet lies a shield and near the spear is a serpent. This serpent would be Erichthonius. On the pedestal is the birth of Pandora in relief.[25]

Plato mentions in passing that the eyes, face, hands, and feet were made of ivory, while the middle parts of the eyes were made of stone that was similar to ivory.[26]

We have seen that Phidias' Athena Laches uses an animal skin as the aegis. Here, by contrast, the aegis is a shield with an archaic head of the gorgon in the center and a relief showing a battle of Greeks and Amazons surrounding the gorgoneion. A large fragment of a Roman copy of this shield survives. Notice Phidias' portrait below and slightly left of the gorgoneion, with both hands held above his head. Though the face is realistic and shows his age, the body is presumably idealized.

An Athenian coin from the third century BC depicts Athena Parthenos but there is not much detail.

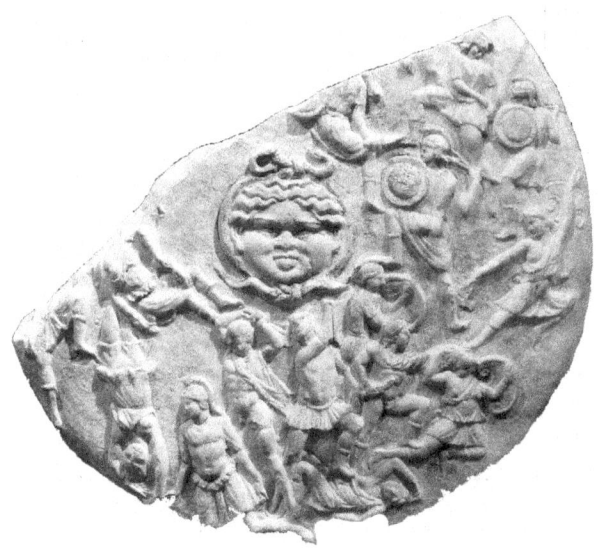

Figure 4-6: Roman Copy of the Shield of Athena Parthenos, British Museum

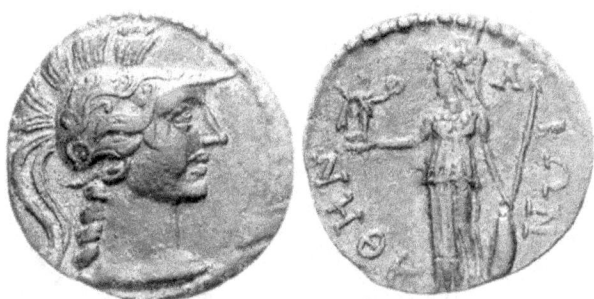

Figure 4-7: Athena Parthenos Shown on an Athenian Coin

Though the ancients were most impressed by huge cult objects made of gold and ivory, such as Athena Parthenos and the Olympian Zeus, the other sculptures of the Parthenon seem more important to the history of art, beginning the long classical tradition.

Parthenon Frieze

The frieze is a sculpture in relief that extends around the entire interior of the Parthenon at the top of the walls. The conventional view is that the frieze represents the Panathenaia, the most important festival of Athens, which included a procession honoring Athena. But some scholars disagree, because it does not include groups that were part of the Panathenaia, such as the *hoplites* (heavily armed soldiers), the *thetes* (those who worked for wages), the *metics* (resident aliens) and others. The frieze obviously represents a procession, but that is the only thing that is certain about it.

Notice how different some of the figures are from Phidias' early statue of Anacreon. They are caught in the middle of action rather than posing in contrapposto position, and they have flowing robes rather than the stiff representation of drapery in the early work. In Figure 4-8, notice the windblown drapery and figures caught in the midst of action.

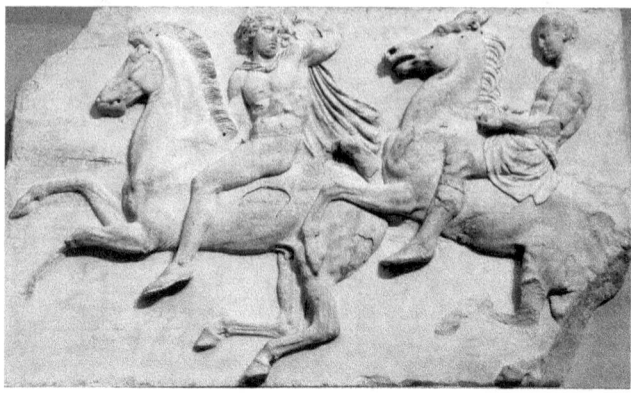

Figure 4-8: Image from the west wall showing part of the cavalcade, British Museum

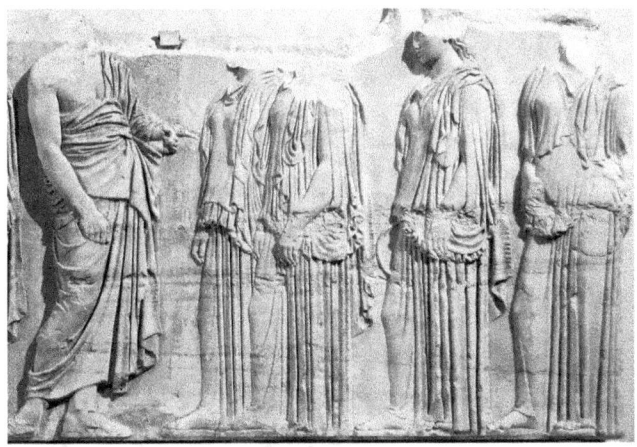

**Figure 4-9: Image from the east wall showing the weavers,
British Museum**

Parthenon Metopes

In Doric Temples, such as the Parthenon, there are triglyphs and metopes under the cornice. The triglyphs are made up of three vertical cuts (triglyph means three-cut) and the metopes are the spaces between them.

In the Parthenon, the metopes were decorated with reliefs of the battle between the centaurs and the Lapiths. According to the myth, King Pirithous of the Lapiths, who lived in the mountains of what is now northern Greece, invited the Centaurs (who were half man and half horse) to his wedding, and because the Centaurs were not accustomed to drinking wine, they got so drunk that they tried to rape the bride and other women there. The Lapiths fought and defeated the Centaurs.

Notice how dynamic the illustrations are, with figures caught in the midst of action—again, a strong contrast with the early figure of Anacreon—and how well they are composed to fit into the square spaces of the metopes.

Parthenon Pediments

The sculptures on the pediments of temples (the triangular areas under the roofline) were considered the most important art

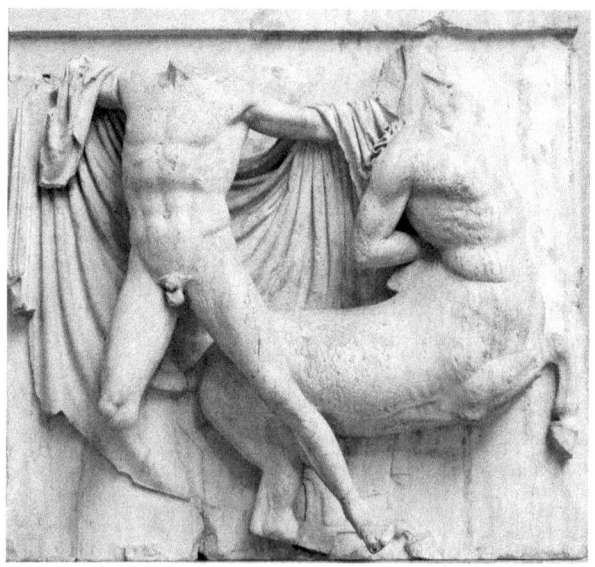

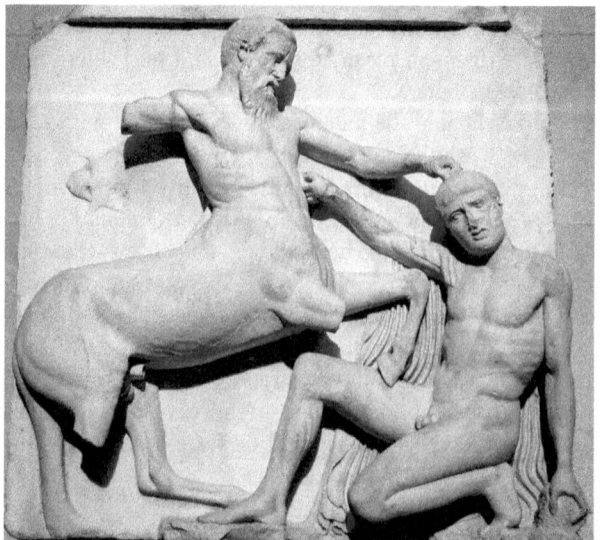

Figure 4-10: Metopes from the Parthenon, British Museum

of ancient Greek temples, apart from the cult object themselves.

The east pediment is the more important pediment of the Parthenon. It shows the birth of Athena. According to the myth, Zeus swallowed Metes after impregnating her because there was a prophecy that she would bear a child who would be more powerful than his father. Then Athena sprang out of the head of Zeus, full-grown, in armor, giving a war cry.

The west pediment shows the contest between Poseidon and Athena for possession of Attica (the region that had Athens as its capital). According to the myth, Athena won by giving Attica the gift of the olive tree.

Individual sculptures that survive more or less intact are interesting because they show the gods as humans in natural positions—not as static icons.

For example, the statue of Dionysus from the east pediment, designed to fit into the corner of the pediment, could be a statue of an athlete relaxing.

Likewise, the sculptures from the other end of the east pediment, sometimes identified as the Three Fates, are also a naturalistic representation of three women relaxing.

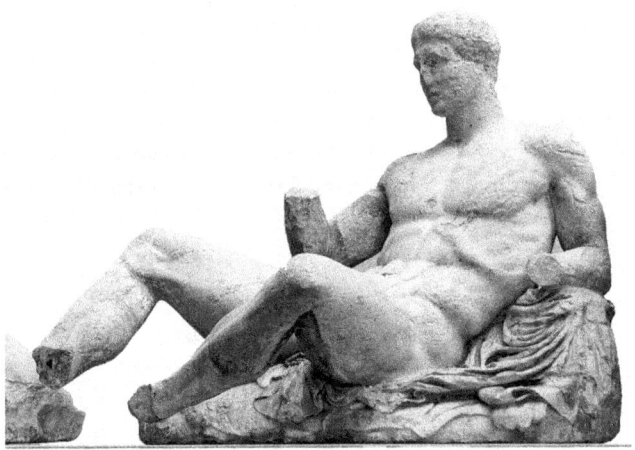

Figure 4-11: Dionysus, British Museum

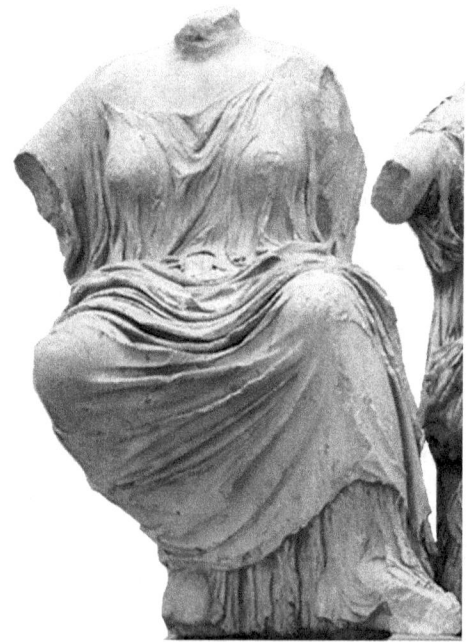

**Figure 4-12: One of the Three Fates,
British Museum**

The Dionysus and Three Fates on the more important east pediment are of such high quality that they are clearly by the most accomplished artists who worked on the Parthenon. Perhaps they are by Phidias himself, though the three fates also look like the one sculpture that we are able to attribute to Phidias' pupil Agoracritus, covered in Chapter 8.

Chapter 5
Myron

Myron was one of the most celebrated classical sculptors in ancient times, but very little is known of his life and very few of his works survive.

He was born in Eleutherae, in Boeotia near the border of Attica (the region with Athens as its capital). He lived most of his life in Athens and was always considered an Athenian. He worked in bronze. He had a son, Lycius, who was also an artist.

Diskobolos (Discus Thrower)

Myron was famous in antiquity and for a statue that is still well known, the Diskobolos, or discus thrower, often referred to using the Latinized spelling Discobolus. The discus thrower is shown at the moment of maximum tension, when he has pulled the discus as far back as he can and is about to change the direction of motion to throw it forward.

The statue was praised in antiquity for its dynamic pose, harmony, and balance, though Pliny had this reservation about it: "though he was very accurate in the proportions of his figures, he has neglected to give expression besides which, he has not treated the hair and the pubes with any greater attention than is observed in the rude figures of more ancient times."[28]

The figure does have a mask-like face with no expression, as Pliny said. As we will see, Myron's statue of Marsyas shows that he was capable of creating facial expressions that show emotion. We can speculate that Diskobolos was an early sculpture, and Myron began focusing on facial expression as well as on dynamic poses only in his later sculpture.

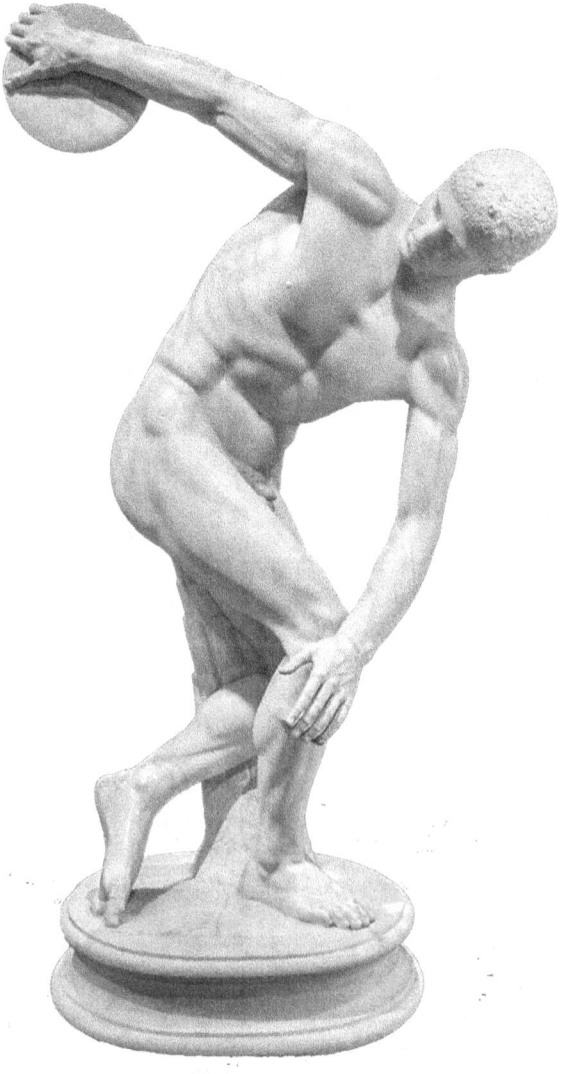

Figure 5-1: Roman copy in marble of the Diskobolos,
National Roman Museum Palazzo Massimo alle Terme.

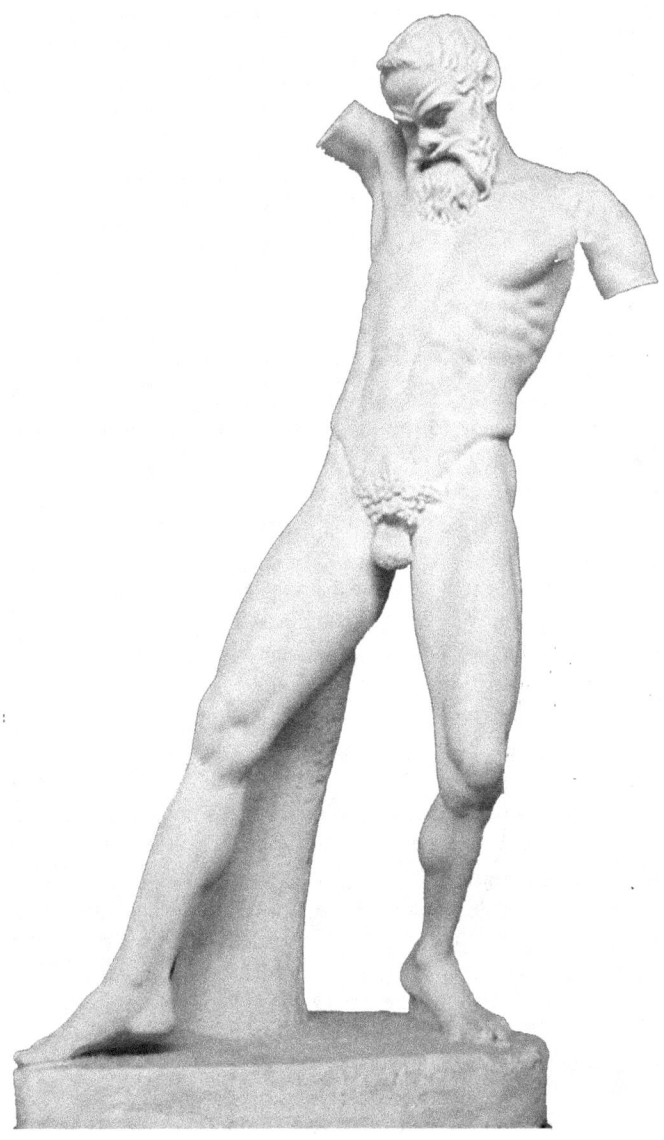

**Figure 5-2: Marsyas the Satyr,
Vatican Museum.**

Marsyas

We also have a Roman copy in marble of Myron's statue of Marsyas the satyr.

According to one version of the myth of Marsyas, Athena invented the flute but threw it away because playing it distorted her face. Marsyas picked it up, learned to play, and challenged Apollo to a musical contest. Marsyas played the flute, making everyone dance in a wild frenzy. Apollo played the lyre so beautifully that everyone stood silently with tears in their eyes. This version of the myth shows the Greek god Apollo, who often represents order and self-control, replacing the more primitive and ecstatic pre-Greek religion.

The statue shows Marsyas at the moment when he has pulled backward in surprise to see the flute lying on the ground before bending down to pick it up, depicting a moment when the figure is about to reverse direction, like the Diskobolos. It shows the satyr's emotion of surprise very clearly, a contrast with the emotionless Diskobolos.

This was originally part of a group that included Athena as well as Marsyas. We can see that Marsyas' posture is dynamic, caught in the midst of action, but we can only imagine how Athena fit into the composition.

Marsyas is the one figure made by this first generation of classical art that shows extreme, uncontrolled emotion. Others have restrained emotions, even when they are in the midst of battle or are dying, showing the virtue that Greeks called *sophrosyne*, which can be translated as self-control or moderation or temperance—controlling one's passions rather than being carried away by them. Satyrs were considered wild and half animal, so they were comic characters who were looked down on. In the Athenian theater, each trilogy of tragedies was accompanied by one satyr play, where the satyrs acted in ridiculous ways.

Theseus and the Minotaur

There are also fragments of a Roman marble copy of another work by Myron, Theseus and the Minotaur. According to the myth, the Athenians had to send seven young men and seven young women to Crete periodically (some say every year, some every seven years, and some every nine years) to be sacrificed to the Minotaur, who was half man and half bull and who lived in the midst of the labyrinth. One year, Theseus, king of Athens, went with the victims and killed the Minotaur. As he approached the Minotaur, he laid down a thread that had been given to him by Ariadne, daughter of King Minos of Crete, who had fallen in love with him, so he was able to escape from the labyrinth by following the thread and then to flee from Crete with Ariadne.

Even in the partial fragments of this statue that we have, the Minotaur seems to be in the midst of the struggle, so it as likely that this work caught the critical moment before Theseus killed him. We can only imagine how Myron would have depicted this more complex scene in the dynamic style of the Diskobolos.

Other works

Pliny says that Myron was "was rendered more particularly famous by his statue of a heifer, celebrated in many well-known lines.... He also made the figure of a dog, a Diskobolos, a Perseus, the Pristae, a Satyr admiring a flute, and a Minerva, the Delphic Pentathletes, the Pancratiasae, and a Hercules [and] . a monument which he erected to a cricket and a locust. He also executed the Apollo ... [that] was restored by the Emperor Augustus, he having been admonished to do so in a dream."[29] The bronze heifer was so celebrated that it there were thirty-six epigrams about it in the Greek anthology, and a collection of these epigrams and other ancient writings about statue takes up nineteen pages.[30] One legend said that the bronze heifer on the Acropolis was so lifelike that a cowherd tried to drive it away.[31]

It is interesting that he did so many subhuman figures, a satyr, heifer, dog, cricket, and locust. But apart from the works we have looked at, all of his works are lost, including the celebrated statue of the heifer. The incomplete fragments of Theseus and the Minotaur remind us of how much we have lost and how little we have of classical art—even of the works of as great an artist as Myron.

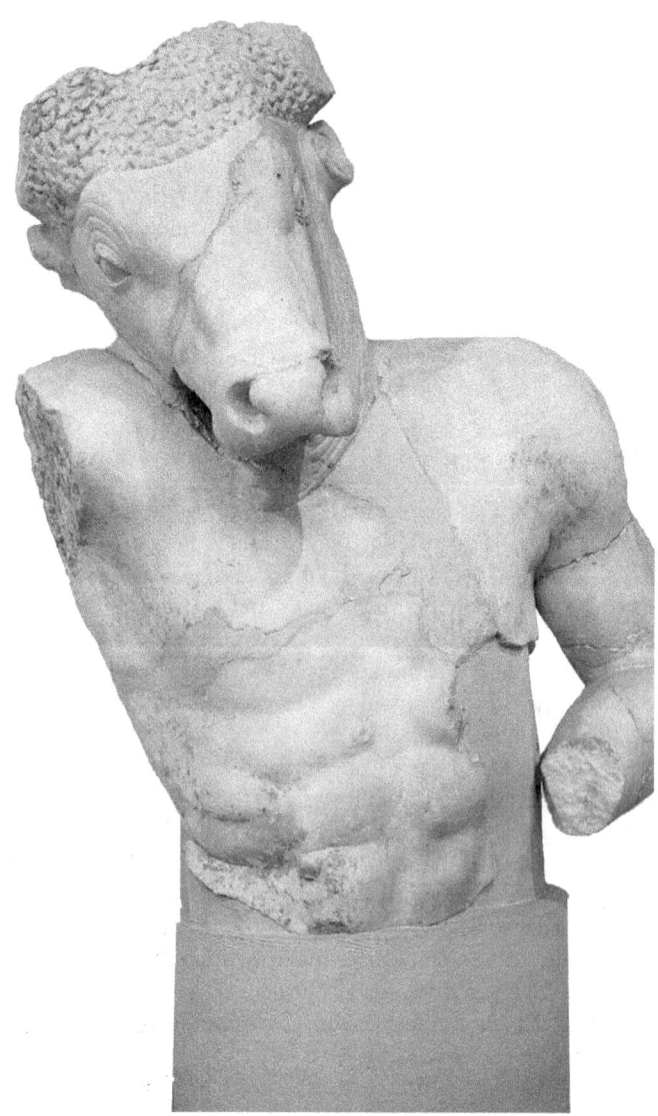

**Figure 5-3: The Minotaur,
National Archeological Museum in Athens**

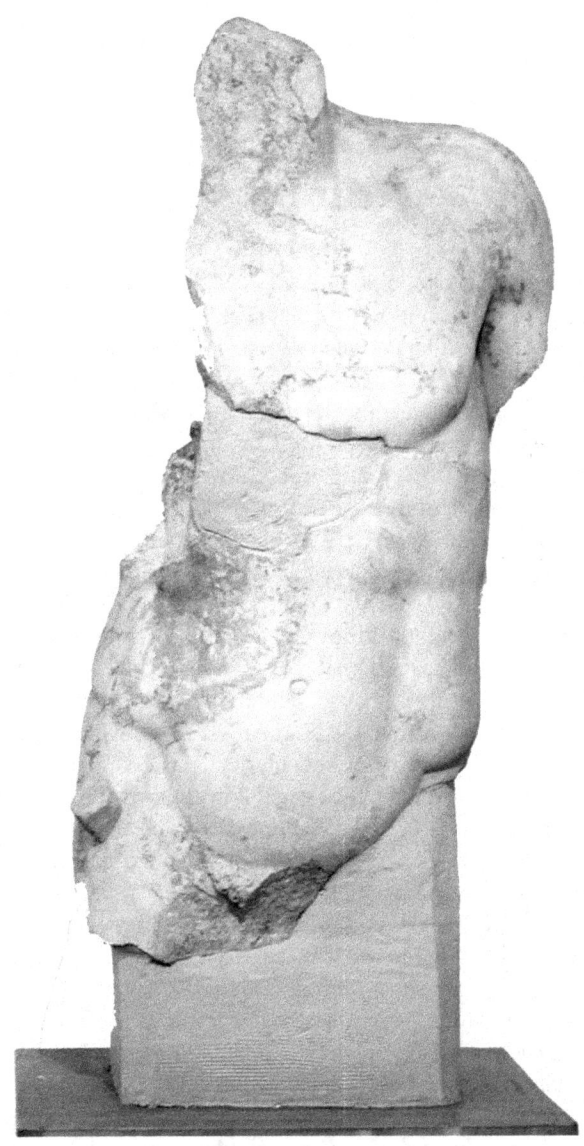

**Figure 5-4: Theseus,
National Archeological Museum in Athens**

Chapter 6
Polyclitus

Polyclitus (Polykleitos) of Argos is one of the three greatest of the first generation of classical artists, along with his contemporaries, Phidias and Myron. He was sometimes called Polyclitus of Sicyon by later authors writing in Latin. The most plausible explanation is that he was born in Sicyon and was given citizenship in Argos as a reward for his accomplishments. His teacher was the Argive sculptor Ageladas.

He was admired as a sculptor in bronze, a sculptor in marble, an architect, and as an artistic metal worker, but only marble copies of his sculptures survive. Most of his works have the same composition: they show a figure standing in the contrapposto position, with weight resting on one leg, like Critius' pre-classical Ephebos and Phidias' early statue of Anacreon.

Polyclitus wrote a treatise defining his idea of the ideal work of art, which was named the "Canon" (Kanon*)*, which means the rule, standard, or measure, Though the treatise is lost, references to it in classical writers indicate that Polyclitus' guiding principles included *symmetria* (which means proper proportion among parts) and *isonomia* (which means equilibrium). We can understand *symmetria* by reading the physician Galen's statement that Polyclitus said beauty depended on "the proportions, not of the elements, but of the parts, that is to say, of finger to finger, and of all the fingers to the palm and the wrist, and of these to the forearm, and of the forearm to the upper arm, and of all the other parts to each other."[32] And we can explain *isonomia* by looking at the balanced poise of Polycleitus' works.

According to one Roman writer, he proved the superiority of his Canon by producing two similar statues, following the Canon to produce one and following the public's suggestions to

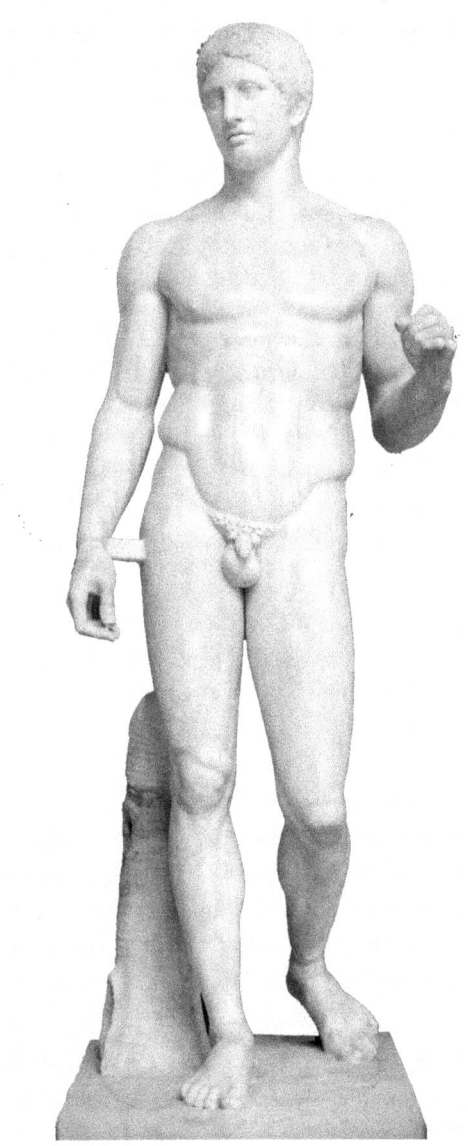

Figure 6-1: Roman Copy of the Doryphoros,
Naples National Archeological Museum.

modify the design of the other. When he showed the two statues to the public, they all admired one and laughed at the other, and Polyclitus told them, "Yet this which you find fault with, you your selves made; this which you admire, I [made]."[33]

Doryphoros (Spear Carrier)

Polyclitus' Doryphoros, which means spear carrier, was bronze, and several Roman copies in marble survive. This statue was such a perfect example of Polyclitus' ideal that it also came to be known as the Canon.

The illustration shows a Roman copy of the Doryphoros that was found in Pompeii. Originally, he was holding a spear in his left hand. The tree stump was added in the marble copy to stabilize the statue but would not have been needed in the bronze original.

The statue is larger than life size, about 6' 11" tall. The proportions are very precise: for example, the body is seven times as large as the head. The body is naturalistic, in the contrapposto position resting on one leg as the subject begins to step forward. The face shows no emotion.

Some later statues, such as the Augustus of Prima Porta (a statue of the Roman emperor Augustus Caesar) use the same proportions and were influenced by this statue by Polyclitus.

Diskophoros (Discus Carrier)

The Diskophoros, oe discus carrier, was also designed based on the proportions of the Canon. Like the Doryphoros, the body is naturalistic and the face shows no emotion. We have a marble copy of the bronze original, with a tree stump added to give it the extra stability needed with marble.

There is a very obvious contrast with Myron's Diskobolos. Polyclitus shows the discus thrower poised and upright, pausing for a moment before throwing the discus, while Myron shows the figure twisted at the point of greatest tension while throwing the discus.

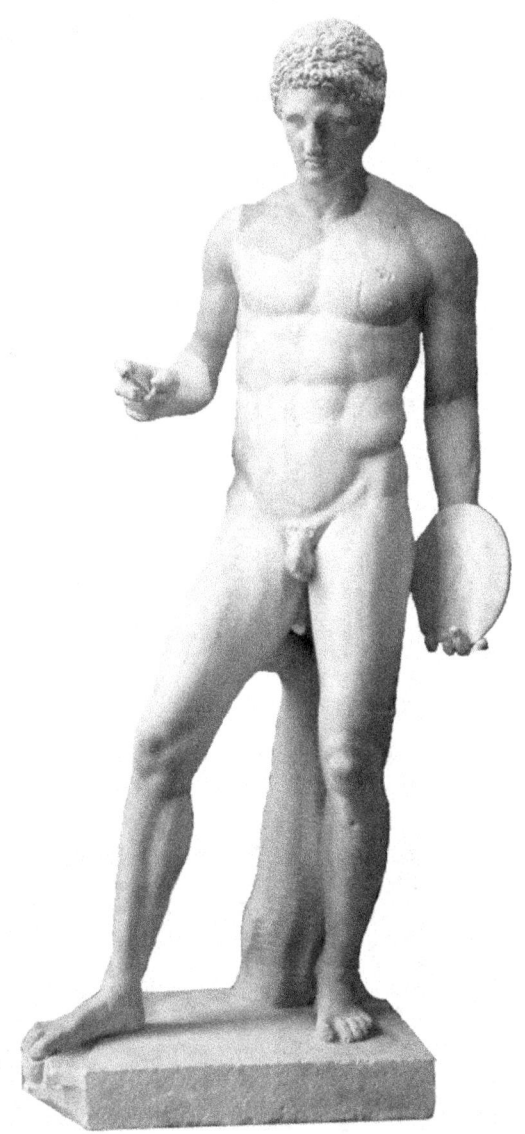

Figure 6-2: Roman Copy of the Diskophoros,
Louvre Museum.

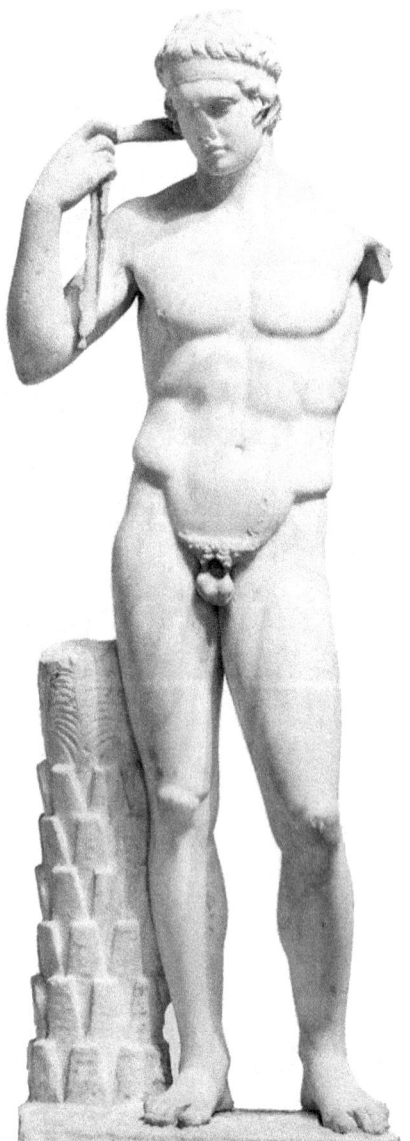

**Figure 6-3: The Farnese Diadumenos,
British Museum.**

Diadumenos (Diadem Carrier)

The diadumenos shows an athlete who has just won a contest and is tying the diadem around his head—a ribbon that identified the winner. As in the typical work of Polyclitus, the figure stands in the contrapposto position and his face shows no sign of emotion.

Many Roman copies in marble of the original bronze statue survive, either in part or almost whole. The Farnese Diadumenos, so called because it was once in the Farnese collection assembled by Cardinal Alessandro Farnese who became Pope Paul III (1534-1549), preserves part of the ribbon. The tree stump would not have been needed in the bronze original. There are several copies of this statue, which look different from each other; we can assume that the original had proportions that followed Polyclitus' Canon.

Wounded Amazon

Pliny mentions a contest held in the mid 400s BC among five sculptors, including Phidias, Polyclitus, and Cresilas, to design a statue of an Amazon for the temple of Artemis of Ephesus, a Greek city in Ionia, on the coast of what is now the Asian part of Turkey, where the cult of the goddess Artemis was connected with the tribe of women warriors called the Amazons. The artists themselves were to judge which was best, and each said his own was best, but all the others agreed that Polyclitus' statue was the second best, so it won the contest.[34] It is impressive that Polyclitus' statue was considered better than Phidias'.

We have copies of several statues of wounded amazons that were probably entries in this contest, and the attribution to the artists is not completely certain, but the illustration shows the statue that was most likely Polyclitus' winning entry that stood in this temple. Again, the pillar added to give stability to this Roman marble copy would not have been needed in the original bronze by Polyclitus

This version of the wounded Amazon is most closely in keeping with Polyclitus' Canon and style. Even though the Amazon is wounded and has left the battle without her weapons, she is standing poised in the contrapposto position and her face

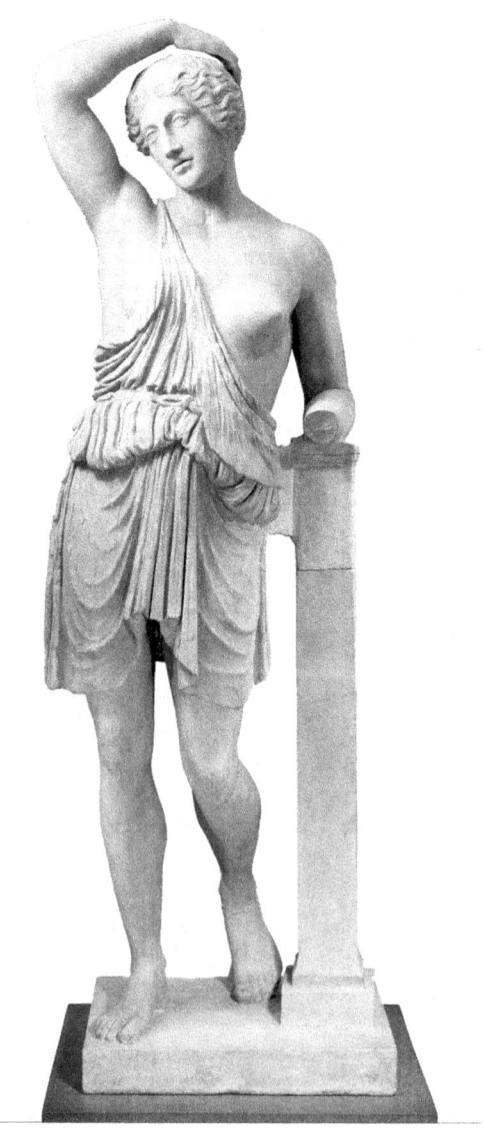

**Figure 6-4: The Wounded Amazon,
Metropolitan Museum.**

shows muted emotion. The one difference from his other statues is that, unlike men, women were not traditionally depicted nude, so this sculpture is the one example we have showing us that Polyclitus was very skilled at depicting drapery.

Hera at the Heraion Near Argos

Polyclitus also produced a huge gold and ivory statue of Hera which was in the Heraion, the Temple of Hera near Argos. According to Strabo, this statue was as beautiful as Phidias' Athena Parthenos and Olympian Zeus, but not as large or as costly. Worship of Hera was central to the religion of Argos.

In 423 BC, in the ninth year of the Peloponnesian War, the old image of Hera was destroyed by a fire in the Heraion caused by the carelessness of Chryses the priestess, who put a lighted torch near the temple's garlands and then fell asleep; when she saw what she had done, Chryses fled from Argos.[35] Polyclitus was called to build a new one because he was greatest sculptor of Argos. Pausanias described this statue: "The statue of Hera is seated on a throne; it is huge, made of gold and ivory, and is a work of Polyclitus. She is wearing a crown with Graces and Seasons worked upon it, and in one hand she carries a pomegranate and in the other a sceptre. About the pomegranate I must say nothing, for its story is somewhat of a holy mystery. The presence of a cuckoo seated on the sceptre they explain by the story that when Zeus was in

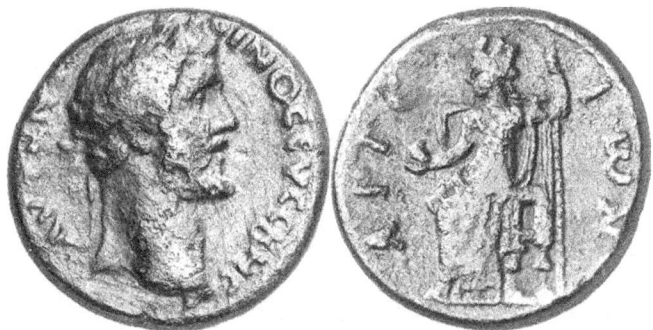

Figure 6-5: Coin Showing statue of Hera at the Heraion

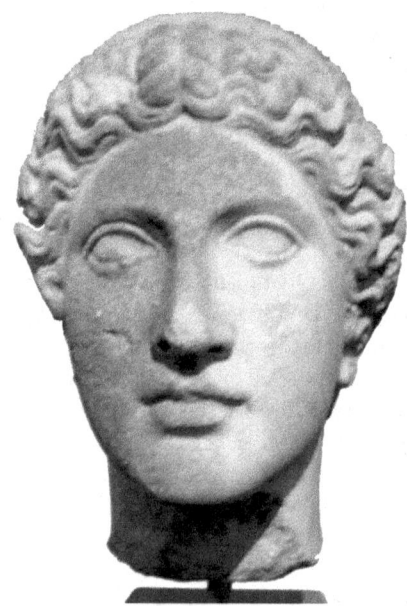

**Figure 6-6: Head of Hera,
Athens Archeological Museum**

love with Hera in her maidenhood he changed himself into this bird, and she caught it to be her pet."[36] A coin from ancient Argos depicts this sculpture.

Though this statue does not survive, nineteenth-century archeologists excavating the Heraion found a smaller head of Hera, which is believed to be by one of the artists who worked on this project as assistant of Polyclitus.

This project was done when Polyclitus was old. Assuming it took 4 years to complete this statue, he was still living in 419 BC.

Other Works

Another famous sculpture by Polyclitus was his statue of two naked boys playing at knuckle bones, called Astragalizontes. Pliny tells us that many considered this work the most perfect example of statuary and that the Emperor Titus put in a conspicuous place in his atrium.[37]

Though the colossal Hera and the Astragalizontes were notable exceptions, most of Polyclitus' statues were figures standing in contrapposto position with proportions following the principles of his Canon.

We have to admire Polyclitus for perfecting this type of sculpture, but his work also seems rather repetitive. Pliny concluded his description of Polyclitus by saying, "It is remarked ... by Varro, that his statues are all ... made very much after the same model."[38]

Chapter 7
Cresilas

Cresilas (Kresilas) was born in Cydonia (Kydonia) on the island of Crete. He studied in Argos as a pupil of Dorotheos of Argos, whom he worked with in Delphi and Hermione. Later, he worked in Athens. It is commonly said that his works are in the style of Myron, but they also seem to have been influenced by the style of Polyclitus and the Argive school. It seems plausible that he was influenced both by his training in Argos and by his career in Athens.

Wounded Amazon

As we have seen, Pliny described a competition between Phidias, Polyclitus, Cresilas, and two other artists to create a statue of a wounded Amazon. This statue is probably Cresilas' entry in the competition. Some attribute it to Polyclitus, but it seems more plausible that Polyclitus did the wounded Amazon that we saw earlier, which has the poised contrapposto stance that is typical of Polyclitus.

Notice that Cresilas' statue, with its arms making a dramatic gesture, is not as static as Polyclitus' Wounded Amazon and not as dynamic as Myron's Diskobolos and Marsyas. In fact, the body and legs are in the contrapposto position typical of Polyclitus while the gesture of the arms and tilt of the head add a dynamic feel reminiscent of Myron.

Notice also that the face is mask-like, similar to Myron's Diskobolos. It is plausible that this is also an early work and that Cresilas, like Myron, did not concentrate on the facial expression until later in his career.

Many subsequent artists made statues with of wounded Amazons with this sort of a stance, which became known as the Sosikles type of wounded Amazon statue.

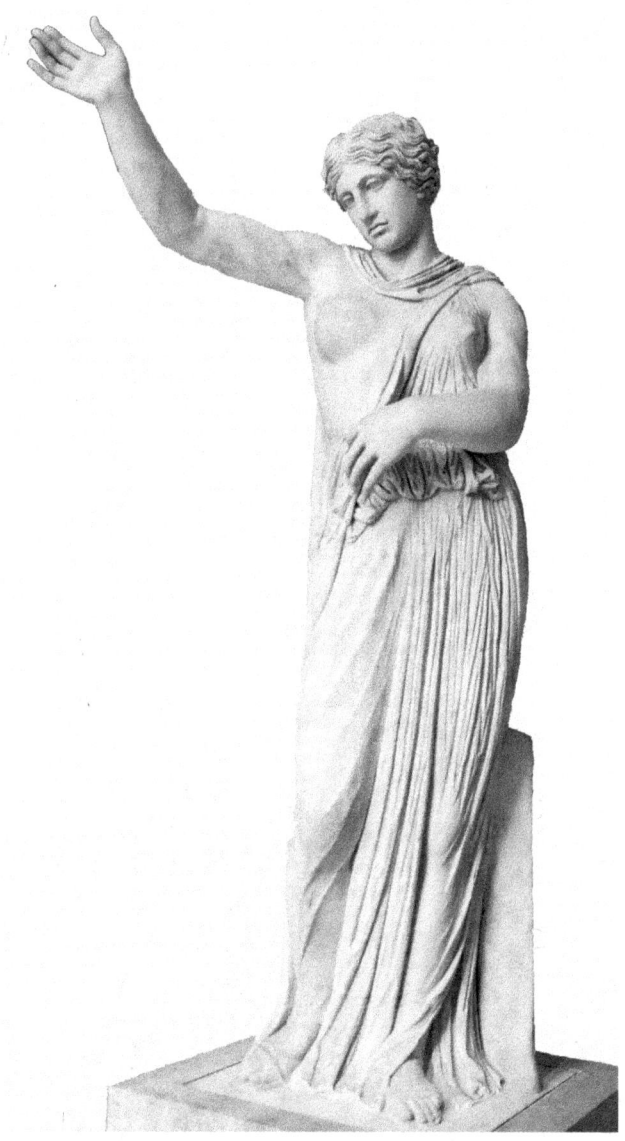

Figure 7-1: Wounded Amazon of the Sosikles Type,
Louvre Museum

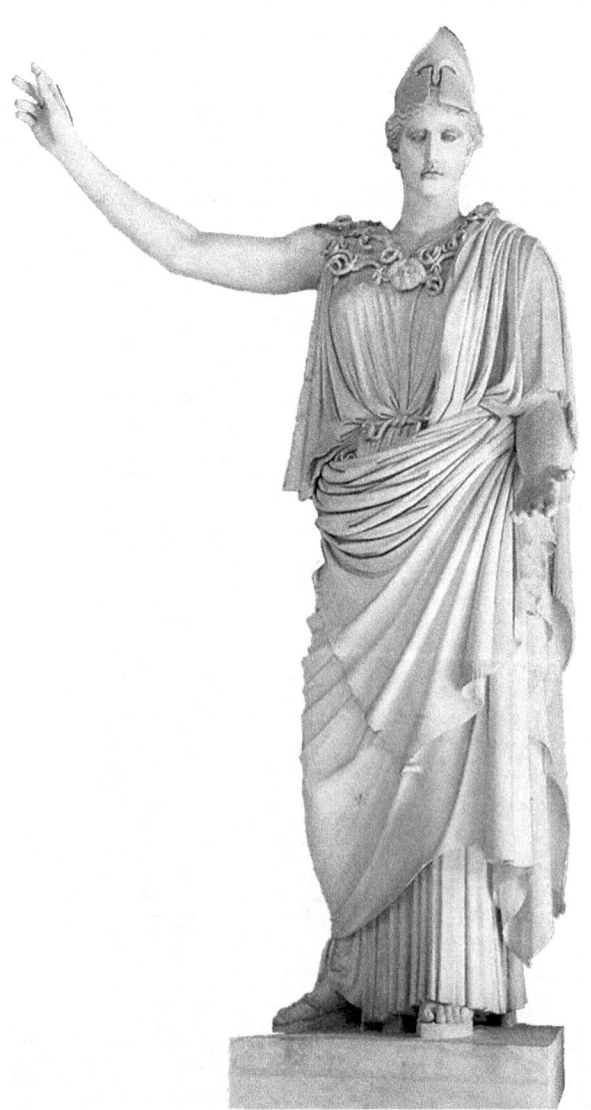

**Figure 7-2: Athena of Velletri,
Louvre Museum**

Athena of Velletri

This Roman statue is probably a copy of a bronze Athena by Cresilas.

Scholars say it is by Cresilas and done shortly after his Pericles because the shape of the face, eyebrows, and nose are similar to his Pericles—and obviously the shape and position of the helmet also are. The similarity is evidence that the two statues are by Cresilas, but it does not say anything about the order in which they were done. This Athena might have come first and influenced the Pericles.

It seems more plausible that the Athena came first, because it has the same mask-like expressionless face as the Wounded Amazon. It is also similar to the Wounded Amazon in having the body in contrapposto position and having the arms making a dramatic gesture, showing the influence of both Polyclitus and Myron.

Like the Wounded Amazon, this statue inspired many subsequent artists who did not copy it but did statues of Athena in similar stances, which became known as the Athena of Velletri type.

Statue of Pericles

In 440-430 BC, Cresilas created a bronze statue of Pericles wearing a Corinthian helmet, which Pausanias says that he saw in the Acropolis, just beyond its monumental entrance (called the Propylea).[39] Several Roman copies or derivative works in marble survive, but rather than being the full statue, they just represent the head without the body, and no one knows whether Pericles was clothed or naked in the original. These Roman copies are often reproduced in books about classical Athens, because they are the only surviving portraits of Pericles.

Judging from the other two works of Cresilas that we have copies of, we can speculate that Pericles was perhaps waving an arm to emphasize a point while orating.

In three of the four surviving copies, you can see hair through the eyeholes of the helmet, higher than where hair would normally

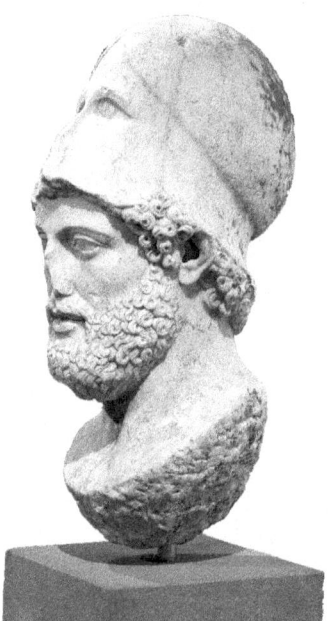

Figure 7-3: Roman copy of the head of Pericles, Vatican Museum

be. It is said that Pericles wore the Corinthian helmet because his head was deformed and was hiding the deformity. Sometimes, comic dramatists of his time called him *schinokephalos* (which means "leek-head" or "squill head."[40]

Here, the face is not mask-like and expressionless, like the Wounded Amazon or the Athena Velletri.

The face has a expression of calm self-control, like the faces in Phidias' work, in keeping with the ideal of the time. The shift from mask-like faces toward this face that shows definite expression makes us suspect that this is a later and more mature work, done after Cresilas began to focus on the expression of the face as well as on the position of the body.

Part 3
The Transitional Age

During the transitional age, there was art that looked back to the age of Phidias and art that anticipated the age of Praxiteles.

Students of Phidias, Myron, and Polyclitus continued working in their styles. Though they all had many students, the only one whose work survives is Agoracritus a follower of Phidias.

Others during this transitional age developed a sensual style that anticipates the age of Praxiteles. Works by Paeonius and Callimachus survive.

There is also a work by Cephisodus the Elder, late in this period, after the end of the Peloponnesian war, which makes a new use of allegorical figures.

Chapter 8
Agoracritus

Agoracritus (Agorakritos), a favorite pupil of Phidias,[41] was born on the island of Paros.

Pliny tells us that Phidias liked Agoracritus because of he was extremely young—showing that he represents the next generation after Phidias. Pliny also tells us that Phidias gave his own name to many of Agoracritus' works,[42] which makes it hard to attribute specific works to Agoracritus, though he clearly produced some of the sculptures of the Parthenon.

Pausanius and Pliny mention four works by Agoracritus, statues of Zeus, Itonian Athena, and the Great Mother (probably Cybele, an ancient mother goddess) in Athens, and a statue of Nemesis in Rhamnus.[43]

Nemesis of Rhamnus

The one surviving work that we can attribute with confidence to Agoracritus is the Nemesis of Rhamnus.

According to Pliny, the Athenians held a contest between Phidias' two favorite pupils, Agoracritus and Alcamenes, to make a statue of Aphrodite, and they chose the work of Alcamenes, partly because he was a native-born Athenian while Agoracritus was born in Paros. Agoracritus was so angry that he changed the name of his work to Nemesis, the goddess of retribution, and sold it to Rhamnus on the condition that it would never be brought to Athens.[44] Rhamnus was in northeastern Attica and had an archaic sanctuary to Nemesis, who was sometimes called Rhamnusia—that is, the goddess of Rhamnus—because her worship centered there.

Interestingly, Pausanius says that Phidias made the Nemesis of Rhamnus, showing that the works of Phidias' students were

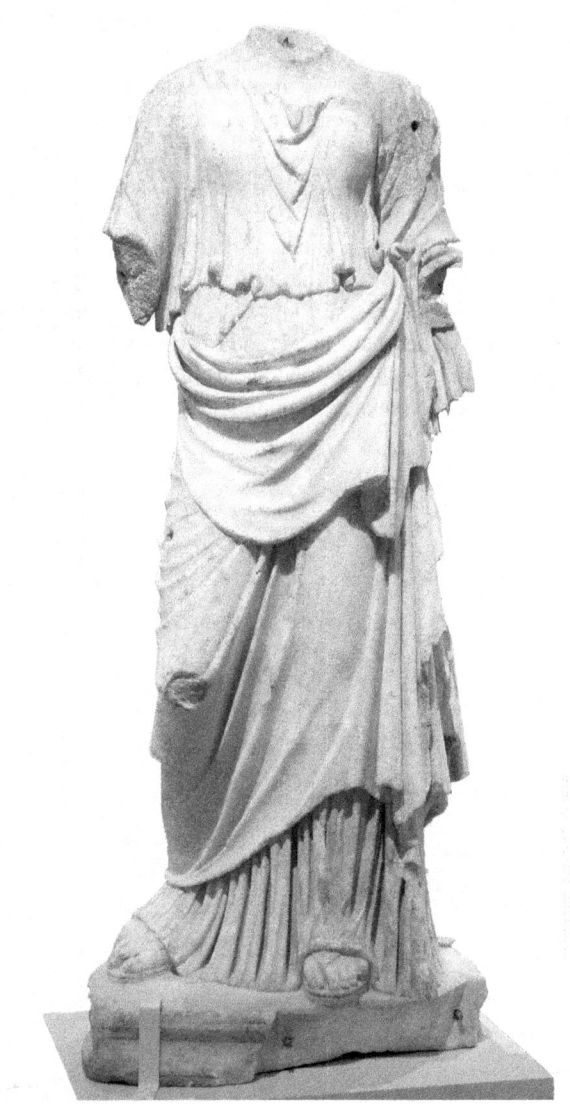

Figure 8-1: Roman Copy of Nemesis of Rhamnus,
Kinsky Palace in Prague.

attributed to Phidias himself. He also described the statue: "on the head of the goddess is a crown with deer and small images of Victory. In her left hand she holds an apple branch, in her right hand a cup on which are wrought Aethiopians."[45]

Agoracritus' Nemesis was destroyed by early Christians, but archeologists have found enough fragments on the site to identify many Roman copies that are smaller than the original and are missing the details that Pausanias described.

The statue is reminiscent of the Three Fates in the pediment of the Parthenon, showing that Agoracritus was working in the style of his teacher. Notice that it is in the contrapposto position, with weight resting on one foot. This was a cult image (used in the temple of Nemesis at Rhamnus) rather than a decorative work, so it gives us a clue that Phidias' cult images, such as the Athena Parthenos, might have also been naturalistic.

Chapter 9
Paeonius of Mende

Paeonius (Paionios) was from Mende in Thrace, a backward district in northern Greece, parts of which began to become Hellenized when Athenian and Ionian colonies were established there before the Peloponnesian War. Mende was part of the Delian League at the beginning of the Peloponnesian War, showing that it was dominated by Athens.

Very little is known about Paeonius' life. Pausanias says he did sculptures in the pediment of the front portico of the Temple of Zeus in Olympia,[46] an important job that implies that his work was admired. Phidias and his workshop created the famous statue of Olympian Zeus for this temple, so Paeonius might have come in contact with them at the time and been influenced by them.

Nike

The one surviving work that can be attributed with certainty to Paeonius is the Nike (Victory) that stood in the sanctuary of the Temple of Zeus in Olympia.

This statue was erected a few years after Athens and its allies defeated Sparta at the Battle of Sphacteria in 425 BC, early in the Peloponnesian War, and was paid for with the spoils of that victory. Pausanias wrote, "the Messenians themselves declare that their offering [this statue] came from their exploit with the Athenians in the island of Sphacteria, and that the name of their enemy was omitted through dread of the Lacedaemonians [Spartans]."[47]

Originally, Nike had a sword in her right hand, wings, and flowing drapery behind her.

The surviving large fragment of the statue was excavated in Olympia in the nineteenth century. It makes very skilled use of

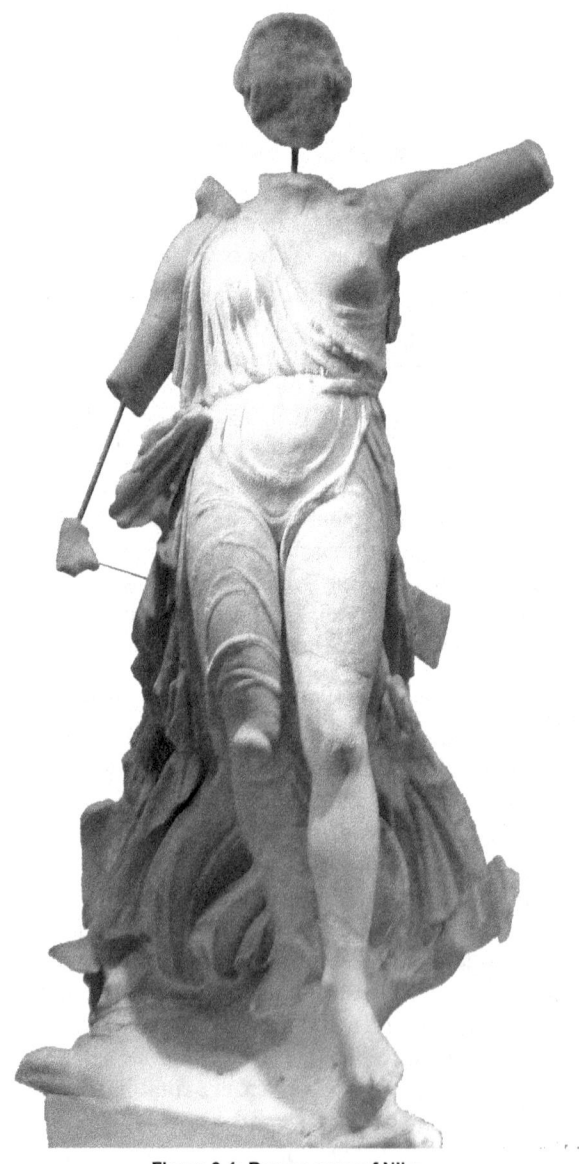

**Figure 9-1: Roman copy of Nike,
Archeological Museum of Olympia**

drapery, with a diaphanous gown that reveals the body underneath and is very sensual. This is called "wet drapery," meant to cover and also reveal the female body. Before this time, female figures were always clothed. During the age of Praxiteles, the first nude female figure appears. This wet drapery represents a transition between the two.

Chapter 10
Callimachus

Callimachus (Kallimachos) was an architect and artist who worked in both Corinth and Athens.

Vitruvius, a first century BC architect and writer, gives Callimachus credit for inventing the Corinthian column when he was working in Corinth and happened to see a tomb that an acanthus plant had grown on.[48] This is the most ornate of the classical columns, with two rows of acanthus leaves on its capital, and it was the basis of one of the three most important orders of classical architecture: Doric, Ionic, and Corinthian.

Pausanias says that Callimachus, "although not of the first rank of artists, was yet of unparalleled cleverness, so that he was the first to drill holes through stones." Perhaps Callimachus did this because the elaborate capital of the Corinthian column required some drilling of the stone, though some say that Pausanias meant that Callimachus drilled holes to create details of his works, such as hair and foliage.[49]

Pliny tells us that Callimachus was known for "being always dissatisfied with himself, and continually correcting his works … affording a memorable example of the necessity of observing moderation even in carefulness," and that he ruined his Laconian Female Dancers by excessive correctness.[50]

Apparently, he was also a bit of an inventor. Pausanias says that he created a golden lamp dedicated for Athena Parthenos that would burn day and night for an entire year if filled with oil: "The wick in it is of Carpasian flax [perhaps asbestos] the only kind of flax which is fire-proof, and a bronze palm above the lamp reaches to the roof and draws off the smoke."[51]

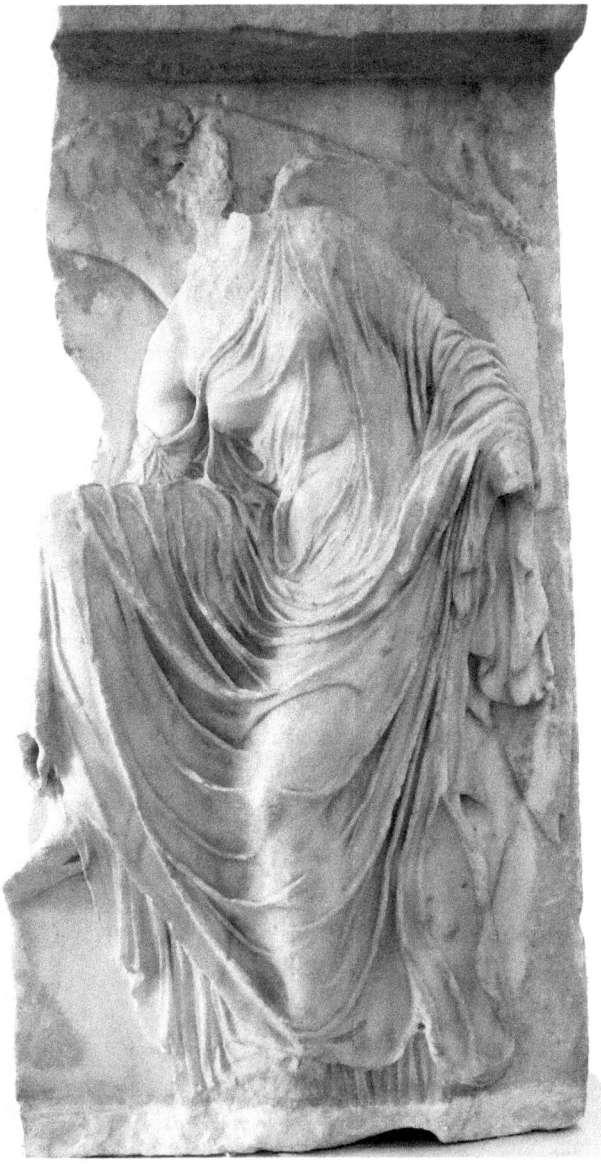

**Figure 10-1: Nike Adjusting Her Sandal,
Acropolis Museum**

Nike Adjusting Her Sandal

One of his works survives in the original: the relief of Nike Adjusting Her Sandal from the frieze of the Temple of Athena Nike on the Acropolis in Athens, which was completed in 410 BC. This work was created a bit later than Paeonius' Nike but also during the Peloponnesian war and also featuring "wet drapery."

Maenads

Other works that survive in Hellenistic and Roman copies are four reliefs of Maenads dancing in a frenzy. Maenads were women who followed Dionysus, the god of wine, in myth and who participated in his wild and sometimes destructive rites in historical times. The Romans called the god Bacchus and called the women Bacchantes. The originals of these reliefs may have been in a temple of Dionysus or may have had something to do with Athenian theater, which performed during the festival of Dionysus.

These reliefs also feature "wet drapery" and are very sensual. The woman's body can be seen clearly under the drapery.

Greek art going back to the Kouros and Kore figures depicted naked men and clothed women. Wet drapery, used by Paeonius and Callimachus during the Peloponnesian War, is the first move toward depicting naked women, a move toward the sensual style that became common after the end of the Peloponnesian War.

Venus Genetrix: Doubtful Attribution

The Venus Genetrix is sometimes attributed to Callimachus because of its wet drapery, but this attribution is probably incorrect. Wet drapery is found in both Paeonius and Callimachus; it was probably common at the time, since it is transitional between earlier clothed women and later naked women. All of Callimachus' works that we have are very dynamic compositions, women caught in the midst of motion, while Venus Genetrix is a static composition, standing in the contrapposto position. There

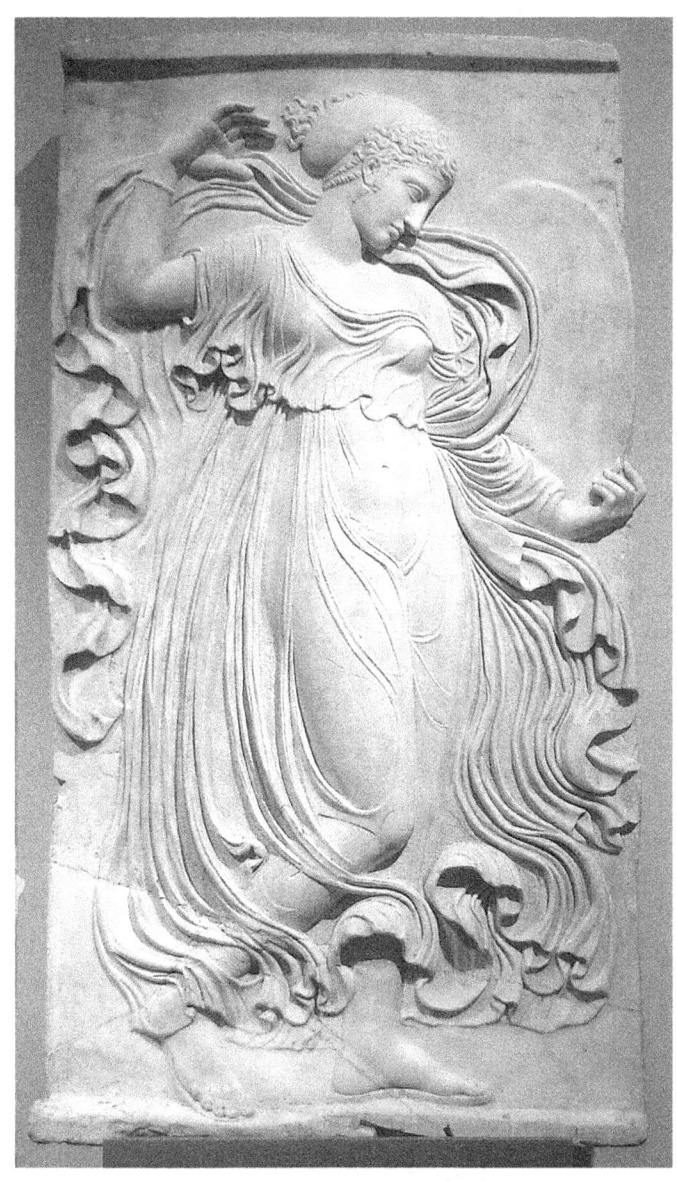

Figure 10-2: Roman copy of Dancing Maenad,
Prado Museum

is no reason to attribute it to Callimachus purely because of its drapery.

Chapter 11
Cephisodotus the Elder

Cephisodotus (Kephisodotos) the Elder is presumed to be the father or uncle of Praxiteles, because Greeks often handed names and occupations down through the family, and Praxiteles had a son with had the same name, Cephisodotus the Younger, a sculptor with no surviving works. The sister of Cephisodotus the Elder was the first wife of Phocion,[52] a statesman who was reelected general a record forty-five times, so he clearly had influential family connections.

Cephisodotus made a statue of Hermes carrying the infant Dionysus, as did Praxiteles.[53] He made a statue of Athena that was in the Piraeus (the port of Athens),[54] probably done after the Piraeus was restored in 393 BC. He also did statues of the muses that were on Mount Helicon,[55] and of Zeus Soter (Zeus Savior) for the city of Megalopolis, which showed Zeus seated on a throne with Artemis standing on his left and an allegorical figure of Megalopolis on his right;[56] Megalopolis was the first major city in Arcadia, founded between 371 and 368 BC by the Arcadian League, in an attempt to resist the power of Sparta after the Peloponnesian War.

Eirene Bearing the Infant Ploutos

His one surviving work is Eirene Bearing the Infant Ploutos (Peace Bearing the Infant Wealth). We have a Roman copy of this statue that is a "point copy," a copy made with a measuring instrument.

This statue personifies abstract ideas, expressing the hope that the peace following the Peloponnesian War will bring prosperity. It was created for Athens and set up on the Areopagus. Drawings of it were included on amphorae (large jars with narrow necks and

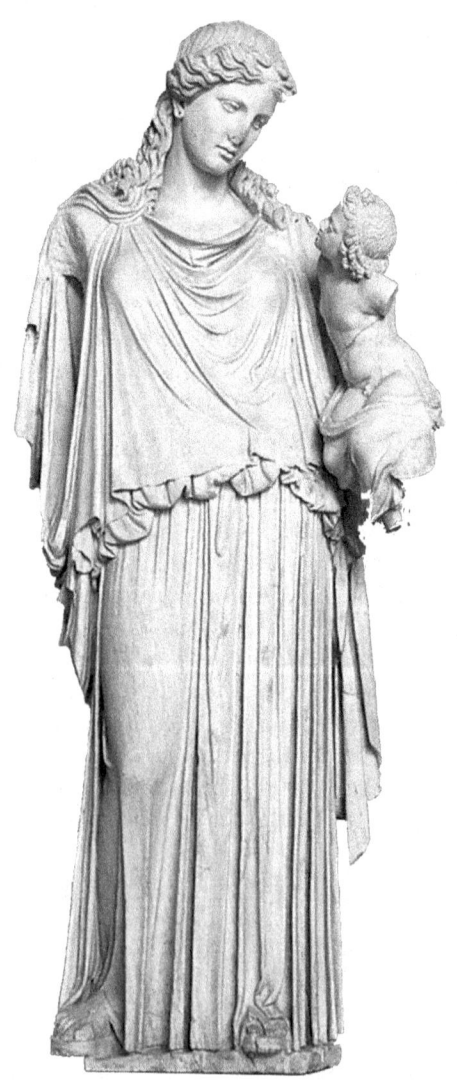

Figure 11-1: Roman Copy of Eirene Bearing the Infant Ploutos, Glyptothek, Munich

two handles) that won Panathenaic prize and that have the name of the Athenian archon of 360-359, which means it must have been created before that date.[57] Pausanias wrote about it, "clever ... was the conception of Cephisodotus, who made the image of Peace for the Athenians with Wealth in her arms"[58].

The innovation, creating new allegorical figures in response to historic events, had great influence through the millennia, and it was popular in the Beaux Arts sculptures in America at the turn of the twentieth century. But in this work, Cephisodotus handles the drapery less skillfully than Agoracritus and many other classical sculptors, and the figures seem a bit stiff and artificial, as they often do in this sort of allegorical sculpture.

Unfortunately, the allegorical message also did not prove true. After losing the Peloponnesian War, Athens never recovered its pre-war wealth and power.

Part 4
The Age of Praxiteles

In this generation, as in the Golden Age, sculpture was centered in both Athens and Argos. Praxiteles and Scopus were the foremost sculptors of the second Attic school, successors to Phidias and Myron, who were foremost in the first Attic school. Lysippus was foremost in the second Argive school, successor to Polyclitus, who was foremost in the first Argive school. And we will see that both schools changed in similar ways.

Chapter 12
Praxiteles

Praxiteles of Athens was considered one of the two greatest classical sculptors, along with Phidias, and the greatest sculptor of his time. He worked in both bronze and marble, but his most famous sculptures were in marble.[59] None of his originals survive, but we do have later copies of his works.

Little is known about his life, neither his teacher nor his country of origin. We do know that he worked mostly in Athens and became a citizen of Athens.

Pliny dates him to the 104th Olympiad (364-360 BC).[60] Pausanias dates one of his works to two generations after Alcamenes,[61] who was Phidias' disciple, and this date is consistent with Pliny's date. Scholars speculate that he was no longer working at the time of Alexander the Great because Alexander did not commission him to do any statues.

Rumors have persisted since ancient times that he had an affair with the courtesan Phryne, who was his model when he created the Aphrodite of Cnidus (Knidos). Phryne's real name was Mnesarete, which means "remembering virtue," but she was called Phryne, which means toad and was a common nickname of courtesans and prostitutes. She was most famous for her trial for impiety, where she was defended by Hyperides (Hypereides), who was one of her lovers. According to one account, when the trial seemed to be going unfavorably, Hyperides had Phryne bare her breasts and ask for mercy, inspiring so much pity among the jurors that they acquitted her, afraid to offend Aphrodite by condemning her priestess. According to another account, she just grasped the hand of each juror and asked for pity, and so was acquitted.[62]

Praxiteles' works are very different from Phidias'. His figures are thinner and are in sinuous poses that make the statues more sensual.

We can speculate on how his work developed by looking at his surviving statues. The Aphrodite of Thespiae and Hermes and the Infant Dionysus are less of a departure from earlier sculpture than his other surviving works, so it is plausible that they were more youthful works, before his own style was fully developed.

Aphrodite of Thespiae

A Roman statue of Venus, dating to the late first century BC, was discovered, broken in several pieces, by workers digging a well in Arles, France in 1651, and it was given to Louis XIV in 1681. The royal sculptor, Francois Girardon, restored it and added two attributes of Venus, the mirror in the right hand and the apple in the left hand. Girardon also refinished the surface of the statue, slimming the figure.

In 1893, the scholar Adolf Furtwängler identified this statue as a copy of the Aphrodite of Thespiae, which was an early work of Praxiteles,[63] perhaps from the 360s BC. This attribution is reasonable. since the statue has the sensual sinuous body that is typical of Praxiteles' work, and the head is strikingly similar to the head of the Aphrodite of Cnidus.

This semi-nude statue, imitated in Hellenistic works such as the Venus de Milo, was a youthful first step toward Praxiteles' fully nude Aphrodite of Cnidus.

Hermes and the Infant Dionysus

Pausanias says that the Temple of Hera in Elis had a statue by Praxiteles of Hermes carrying the infant Dionysus.[64] According to the myth, Dionysus' mother Semele asked his father Zeus if she could see him in all his glory, but seeing him killed her, leaving the infant Dionysus without anyone to care for him. Hermes lifted the infant and took him to the nymphs of Nysa so they could raise him. In this statue, Hermes is stopping to rest on way to Nysa.

The statue was discovered in 1877 in the ruins of the Temple of Hera during an archeological dig in Olympia, Elis, where the ancient Olympic Games were held and where Phidias' famous

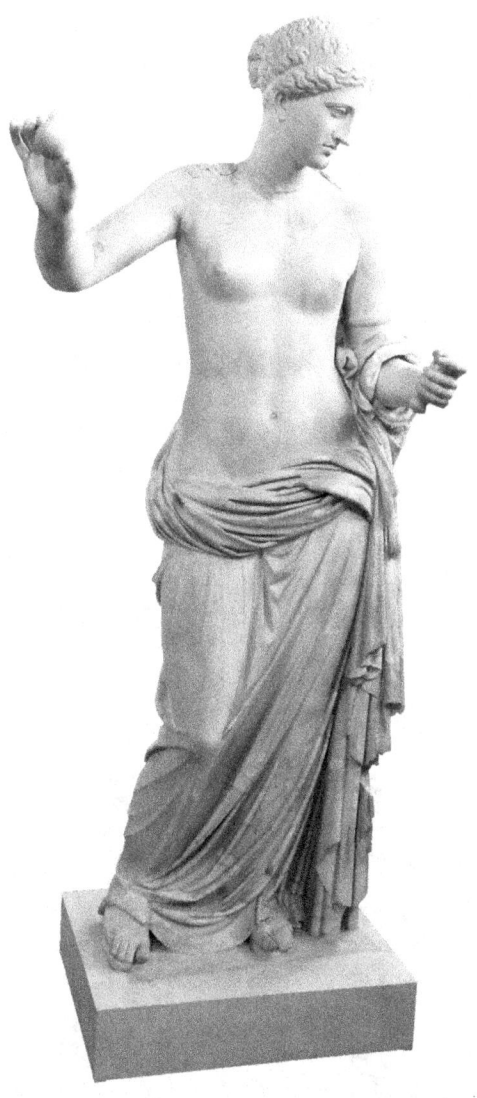

**Figure 12.1: Venus of Arles, Copy of Aphrodite of Thespiae,
Louvre Museum**

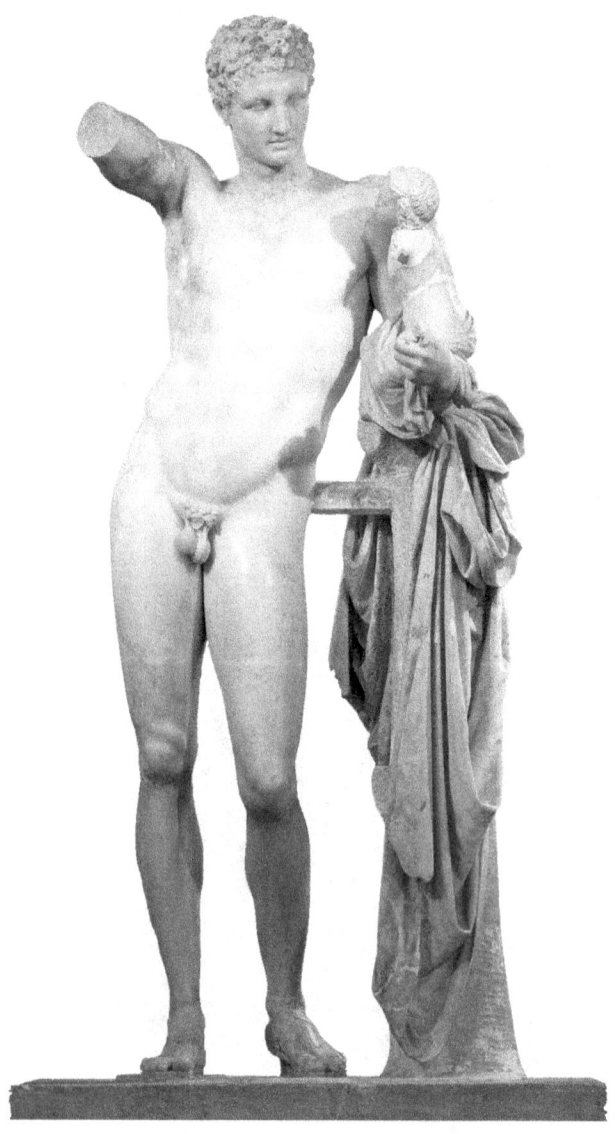

Figure 12-2: Hermes and the Infant Dionysus,
Archeological Museum of Olympia

statue of Olympian Zeus was in another temple. Some scholars say it is an original work of Praxiteles, some say it is a Hellenistic copy, and some say it is a Roman copy.

The infant is held in Hermes' left hand and rests one hand on Hermes shoulder. Hermes' right hand may be holding up something for the infant to look at, perhaps showing a cluster of grapes to the infant who will be the god of wine. The infant's head looks like the head of a child or a small head of an adult, rather than like the head of a baby.

Hermes stands in contrapposto position but his left arm leans on a support, so his body is more sinuous than most contrapposto statues, which is typical of the style of Praxiteles. But Hermes is more hefty than the other figures by Praxiteles, with the body of an adult rather than of an adolescent, though it seems his body is not quite hefty enough to measure up to the standard prescribed by the Canon of Polyclitus. We can speculate that this is an early work by Praxiteles, still influenced by the statues of the golden age, since it does not yet have the slender proportions of his mature works, though it does have their sinuous stance.

It illustrates a scene from a myth, while the later works are actually scenes from everyday life, though they ostensibly depict gods and goddesses.

Aphrodite of Cnidus

The Aphrodite of Cnidus (Knidos) was Praxiteles' most famous work. There are many copies. The illustration is a Roman copy with head, arms, legs, drapery and jug restored. There are several Roman copies that are slightly different from each other; the illustration of a coin from Cnidus shows the original posture, which is more full-figured and is leaning forward a bit more than the Roman copy in the illustration.

This is the first classical statue of a female nude. According to Pliny, Praxiteles did two statues of Aphrodite, one clothed and one naked. The city of Cos (Kos) purchased the clothed one because they considered the nude indecent. The city of Cnidus purchased the nude statue and became famous for it. At a later time, King Nicomedes tried to purchase the statue and offered to pay off the

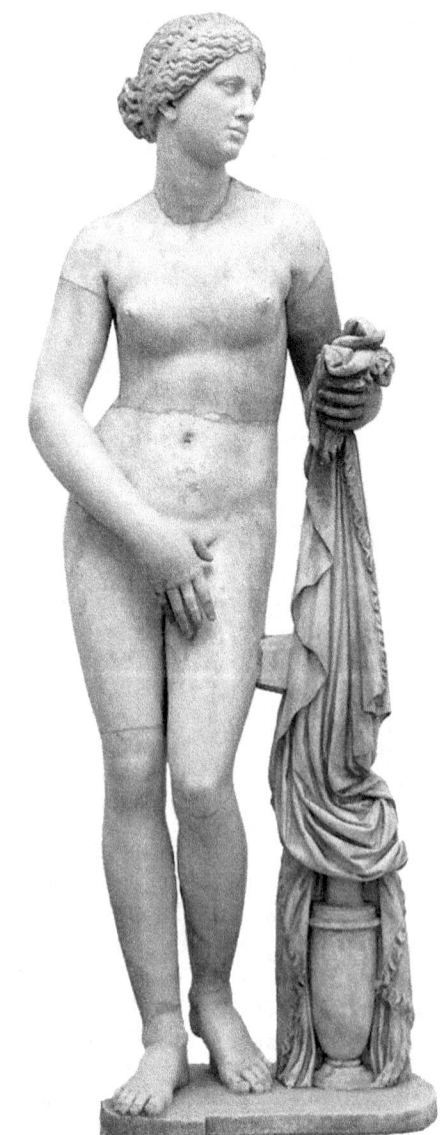

Figure 12.3: Roman Copy of Aphrodite of Cnidus,
Museo Nazionale Romano di Palazzo Altemps

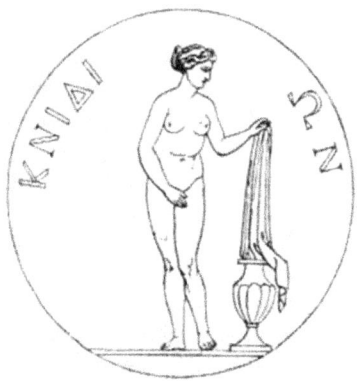

Figure 12-4: Coin showing Aphrodite of Cnidus

entire public debt of Cnidus, but the city refused, unwilling to give up the statue that made it famous.[65]

Aphrodite is apparently either picking up her robe right after leaving the bath or putting down her robe just before entering the bath; she protects her modesty by using one hand to cover her pubic area. This slightly embarrassed nudity earned the statue the name of *Venus Pudica*, the ashamed Venus.

This embarrassment is not the reaction we would expect from a goddess. The earlier Aphrodite of Thespiae is a much more conventional picture of a goddess, self-possessed and unashamed. Though the Aphrodite of Cnidus was used as a cult image, it is actually more like a genre scene, a scene from ordinary life. The statue acts like a mortal woman, not like a goddess, and the attempt to protect her modesty makes the statue even more sensual.

The statue was installed as a cult image in the temple of Aphrodite in Cnidus, and it also became a tourist attraction, as people traveled there specifically to see it. A writer using the name of Lucian tells us that he visited it with a friend, and when his friend saw it, "he ran up and, stretching out his neck as far as he could, started to kiss the goddess with importunate lips."[66] Pliny tells us, "A certain individual, it is said, became enamoured of this statue, and, concealing himself in the temple during the night, gratified his lustful passion upon it, traces of which are to be seen

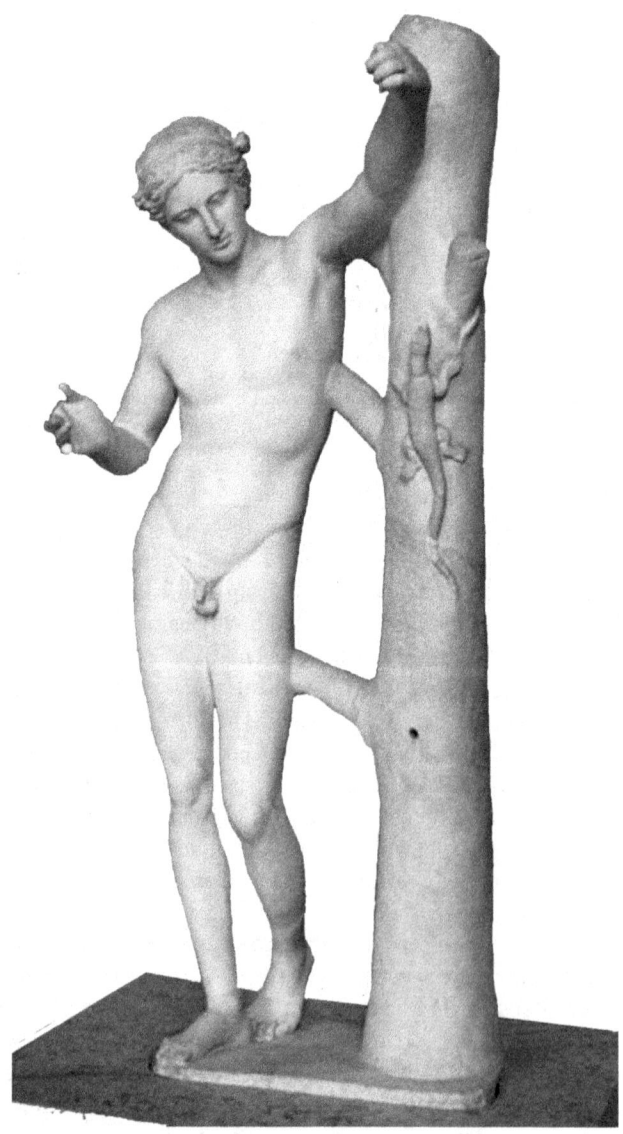

Figure 12.5: Roman Copy of Apollo Sauroktonos,
Louvre Museum

in a stain left upon the marble,"[67] and several other ancient sources tell the same story. This story is obviously a myth, like the story that Myron's bronze heifer was so realistic that a cowherd tried to drive it away, but it emphasizes the sensual appeal of the statue.

Apollo Sauroktonos (Lizard Killer)

There are several 1st and 2nd century Roman copies of Apollo Sauroktonos, which means "Apollo the Lizard Killer," which Pliny says was a work of Praxiteles.[68]

The statue shows Apollo as an early adolescent leaning against a tree and holding his hands in a position that shows he is preparing to catch a lizard that is climbing up the tree. Apollo is very thin, and the body looks even thinner because the head is large in proportion to the body. Though he is standing in contrapposto position, his body curves sinuously because of the way he is leaning against the tree.

It is actually a statue of a scene from the ordinary life of an adolescent rather than a statue of the powerful god Apollo, just as the Aphrodite of Cnidus showed a scene from the ordinary life of a beautiful woman, not a powerful goddess.

The illustration shows a Roman copy that is in the Louvre, which was in the collection that the wealthy Italian Borghese family began in the seventeenth century and which was purchased and brought to France by Napoleon.

Satyr Pouring Wine

There are several Roman copies of Praxiteles' sculpture of a satyr pouring wine from a pitcher into a drinking vessel. The one in the illustration was made in the first century AD and found in 1657 in the villa of the Emperor Domitian at Castel Gandolfo, Italy. The head, right hand, and penis are restorations added in the nineteenth century. Originally, the right hand was holding a wine jug, and the left hand was holding the sort of bowl that the Greeks used for drinking wine, both of which are missing.

It is recognizable as a satyr only by its pointed ears; apart

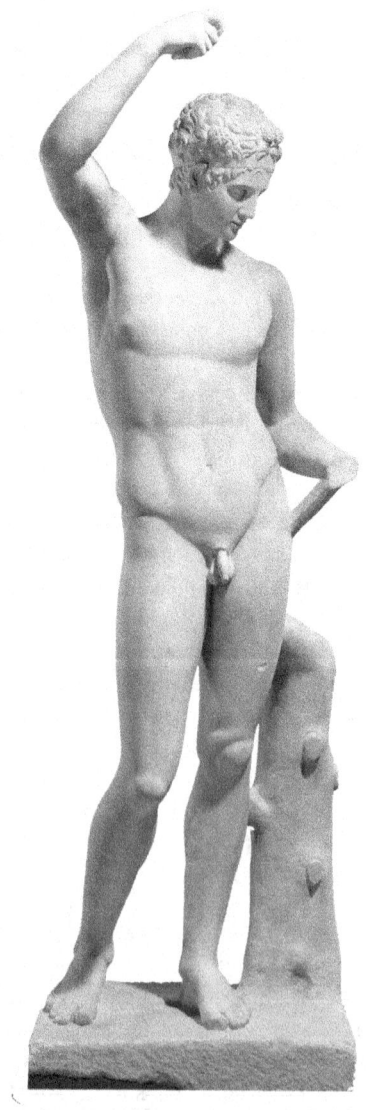

**Figure 12.6: Roman Copy of Satyr Pouring Wine,
J. Paul Getty Museum**

from that, it is one of Praxiteles' typical depictions of everyday life. It also has the adolescent body that is typical of Praxiteles' sculptures. It seems to be standing in contrapposto position, but the body is more sinuous than earlier contrapposto works, also typical of Praxiteles. The position of the arms emphasizes the sinuous stance.

Pausanias tells a story showing that this was one of Praxiteles' favorites among his works:

Phryne once asked of him [Praxiteles, to give her] the most beautiful of his works, and the story goes that lover-like he agreed to give it, but refused to say which he thought the most beautiful. So a slave of Phryne rushed in saying that a fire had broken out in the studio of Praxiteles, and the greater number of his works were lost, though not all were destroyed. Praxiteles at once started to rush through the door crying that his labour was all wasted if indeed the flames had caught his Satyr and his Love [Eros]. But Phryne bade him stay and be of good courage, for he had suffered no grievous loss, but had been trapped into confessing which were the most beautiful of his works. So Phryne chose the statue of Love; while a Satyr is in the temple of Dionysus.[69]

Other Works

Apart from creating works that were copied, Praxiteles created a couple of works that became popular "types." They were not copied directly, but later artists produced works with similar subject matter.

For example, the Apollo Lykeios (Lycean Apollo) was a type that showed Apollo leaning on a tree trunk or tripod with his right arm resting on his head. Praxiteles created the first, which got its name because it stood in Aristotle's school in Athens, called the Lykeion (Lyceum). Later statues of this type are so different from each other that there is no way of knowing what Praxiteles original statue was like.

Another type that originated with Praxiteles was the Satyr Anapauomenos (Resting Satyr), which shows a satyr leaning with his right elbow on a tree trunk, standing on his left leg, with his right leg bent and his right toes touching the ground behind the heel of his left foot. Again, the later statues of this type are so different from each other that they do not let us guess what Praxiteles original was like.

Some works are attributed to Praxiteles on flimsy grounds. It is natural to attribute works to such a famous artist, just as it is natural for Americans to attribute witty quotes to Mark Twain without any basis.

For example, Artemis of Gabii was discovered in 1792. It is identified as Artemis just because of its clothing and is attributed to Praxiteles just because Pausanias said he created a statue of Artemis for the Acropolis. But it is not in Praxiteles' sensual style—the goddess does not stand in the sinuous positions typical of Praxiteles—and the short tunic that it wears is typical of the Hellenistic period, not of Praxiteles' time.

Chapter 13
Scopas

Scopas (Skopas) was born in Paros, an island in the central Aegean Sea that was controlled by Athens. His father was also a sculptor, Aristander of Paros. He travelled and worked in many parts of the Greek world, including working with Praxiteles in Athens, working on the Temple of Athena Alea in Tega in the Peloponnese, and working on the reliefs of the Mausoleum at Halicarnassus in Asia Minor (now Turkey).

Praxiteles and Scopas were the most important artists of the second Attic school of sculpture, as Phidias and Myron were the most important of the first Attic school.

As we will see, some of Scopas' works are reminiscent of the heroic sculptures of the golden age, and others have the more sensual style that became common after the Peloponnesian War. We can speculate, as we did for Praxiteles, that his heroic works came earlier in his career, and his sensual works came later.

Temple of Athena Alea and Head of Hygieia

The Temple of Athena Alea at Tegea in Arcadia was one of the most important shrines of ancient Greece and was famous as a place of refuge for people accused of crimes. The first temple burned down in 394 BC, and Scopas worked on the second temple. To fit this work into his career, we have to assume that work did not begin until decades after the first temple was destroyed.

Pausanias describes this temple:

The modern temple is far superior to all other temples in the Peloponnese on many grounds, especially for its size. Its first row of pillars is Doric, and the next to it Corinthian; also,

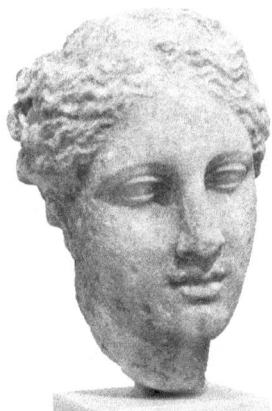

**Figure 13-1: Head of Hygieia,
National Archeological Museum of Athens**

outside the temple, stand pillars of the Ionic order. I discovered
that its architect was Scopas the Parian.... On the front gable is
the hunting of the Calydonian boar. ... On the gable at the back
is a representation of Telephus fighting Achilles on the plain
of the Caicus.[70]

But modern scholars doubt that Scopas was the architect in
addition to doing the decorative sculptures.

Scopas also did a statue of Hygieia, one of the gods and
goddesses of medicine and health, for this temple. Archeologists
found the head of this statue, which is well preserved. It clearly
has the deep-set eyes and almost-open mouth that are typical of
Scopus.

Statue of Meleager

Meleager was the legendary hero who killed a boar that was
terrorizing the people of Calydon. He was also said to have been
one of the Argonauts who accompanied Jason when he sailed on
the Argo to capture the Golden Fleece.

There are many surviving Roman statues of Meleager which
copy the same Greek original, and scholars believe that this

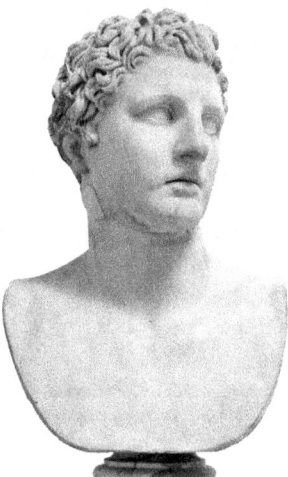

Figure 13-2: Roman Copy of the head of Meleager,
British Museum

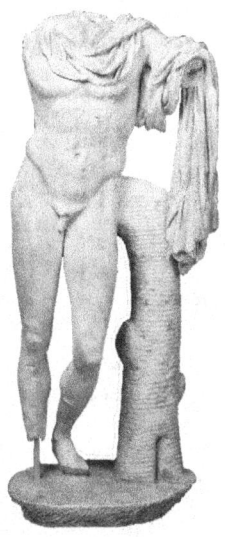

Figure 13-3: Roman Copy of the body of Meleager,
Art Institute of Chicago

original was probably by Scopas. We have seen that Scopas worked on the Temple of Athena Alea and that the east pediment of this temple depicted the story of the Caledonian boar. Pausanias lists Meleager as one of the figures on this pediment,[71] so it is plausible that Scopas created or directed the creation of the sculpture of Meleager for this pediment.

We can get an idea of what the original statue was like from two surviving copies, one of the body and one of the head. It is in the heroic style of the Golden Age and looks something like a typical statue by Polyclitus or the early statues of Phidias, with the same proportions and the figure almost in a contrapposto stance, though it is leaning slightly.

Maenad

Maenads (Bacchantes in Latin) were women who followed the god Dionysus (Bacchus in Latin), the god of wine. Maenad literally means "raving one." Dionysus drove them into an ecstatic frenzy, caused by dancing and intoxication, and they were often destructive and even murderous.

Callistratus (Kallistratos) writing in the third or fourth century AD, described a marble statue of a Maenad by Scopas:

When we saw her face we stood speechless, so clear upon it was the evidence of sense perception, ... so clear was the intimation of Bacchic divine possession stirring Bacchic frenzy .... The hair fell free to be tossed by the wind, and was divided to show the glory of each strand. ... It ... carried a victim [sacrificed animal] ... And the figure of the kid was livid in color, and the stone took on the appearance of dead flesh...[72]

The illustration shows a marble statue found in Marino, Italy, that is generally identified as a copy of this statue by Scopas.

The drapery covers only part of the Maenad's body and is very revealing even where it does cover the body. Like "wet drapery," it displays the female body explicitly without total nudity.

This statue represents a dramatic shift from the heroic figures typical of the Golden Age to the sensual figures that became popular after the Peloponnesian War. The body is sinuous, like

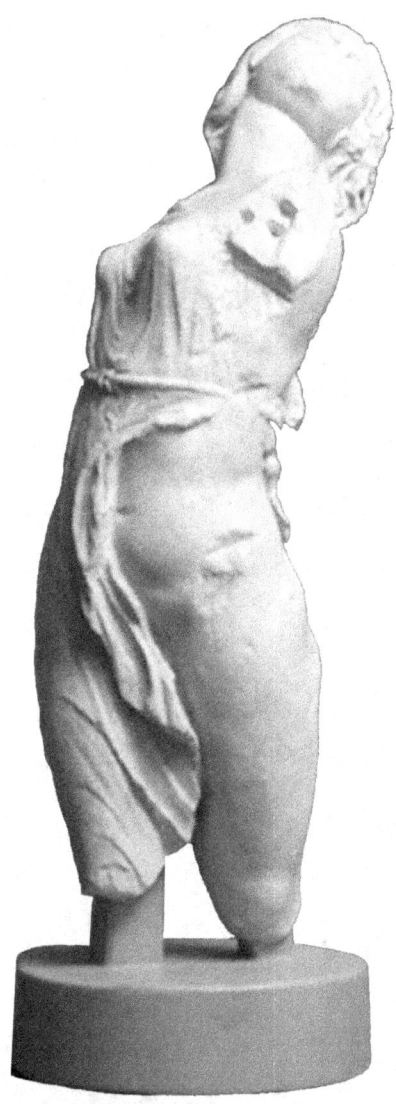

Figure 13-4: Roman Copy of Maenad,
Dresden Albertinum

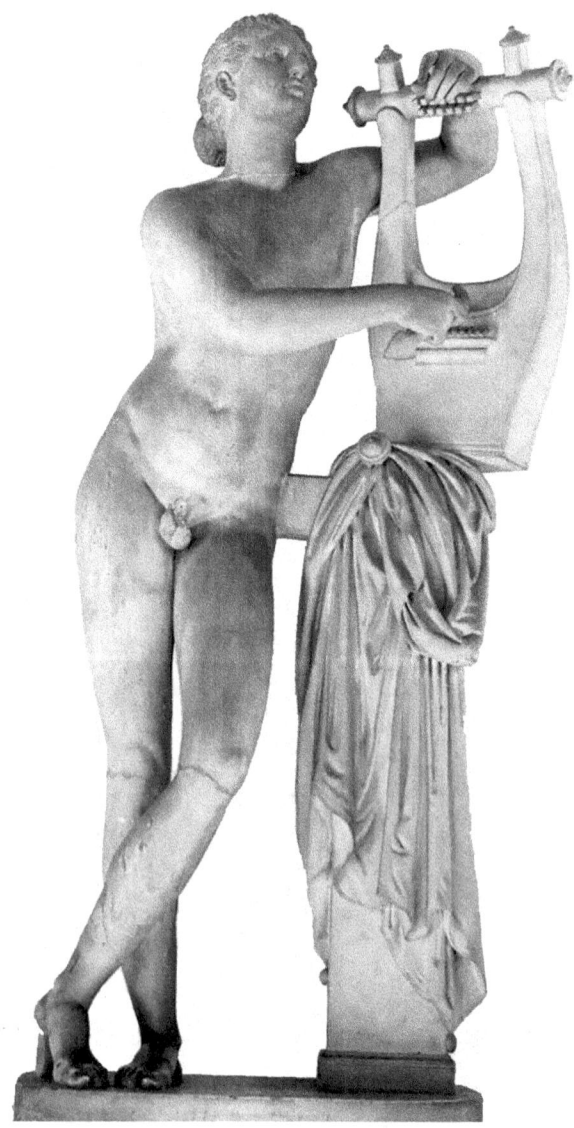

Figure 13-5: Roman Copy of Pothos with Cithara Added,
Capitoline Museum, Rome

the bodies of Praxiteles' sculptures. The clothed female figures of the golden age are replaced by a half-nude female figure. The restrained expressions of the golden age are replaced by an expression that is totally abandoned to emotion.

Pothos (Desire)

The most distinctive thing about the statue of Pothos is its stance, leaning to the right with its feet crossed—looking somewhat unstable, unlike the usual contrapposto stance, which seems very stable. He is a sinuous and delicate figure, reminiscent of the work of Praxiteles, looking upward to express longing, but with his face expressing controlled emotion.

There were many Roman reproductions of the original statue by Scopas, often with different props added. The illustration shows the statue modified by adding a cithara (kithera), changing the sculpture into a representation of Apollo, the god of music, who is often shown playing either a cithara or a lyre.

Pausanias says this statue was part of a group that included three sons of Aphrodite, Pothos (desire), Eros (sexual desire) and Himeros (uncontrolled sexual desire), which were near the Temple of Aphrodite in Megara.[73] Presumably, Pothos is leaning toward the other figures as part of the overall composition of the group.

It is interesting to speculate what the other figures might have looked like. Pothos (desire) is in a languishing pose. Presumably, Himeros would have been in an unrestrained pose, perhaps like the Maenad.

Chapter 14
Lysippus

Lysippus (Lysippos) was born, probably around 390 BC, in Sicyon, which is on the Peloponnese near the isthmus that connects the Peloponnese with the rest of Greece. He became the leading sculptor of the school of Argos and Sicyon. He had a large workshop and many pupils, and there is sometimes doubt about whether works are by him or by a pupil. Lysippus had three sons who were his pupils and became famous artists, Laippus, Boëdas and Euthycrates.

Pliny tells us that he made more works than any other artist,[74] that he kept count of his works by saving one gold piece from his pay for each statue, and that after his death, when the coins were counted, it was found that he had produced more than 1,500 works.[75] He also became the personal sculptor of Alexander the Great.

Lysippus began as a bronze caster. Pliny tells us that he asked the painter Eupompus which of the great artists he should imitate to become an artist himself. Eupompus showed him a crowd of men and told him to imitate nature rather than imitating an artist.[76] But apparently Lysippus did not simply follow nature: he considered the Doryphoros of Polyclitus (the statue that was also called the Canon) to be his model,[77] and he obviously was influenced by Polyclitus' work.

He is the successor to Polyclitus as the greatest sculptor of the Argive school, as Praxiteles is the successor to Phidias as the greatest sculptor of the Attic school. Both Praxiteles and Lysippus broke with their predecessors by moving toward a thinner body type, so we can see that this shift was not confined to Athens but also occurred in Argos and presumably across much of Greece.

Lysippus developed his own canon of ideal proportions, which created thinner figures than the canon of Polyclitus. In addition, Polyclitus' canon had made the head one-seventh as large as the total size of the body, but Lysippus's made the head one-eighth as large, making the statues look taller when people looked up at them (because perspective makes a taller statue appear to have a smaller head). It is interesting that the Argives Polyclitus and Lysippus developed canons of proportions rather than the Athenians, though we expect the Athenians to be the writers and theorists of classical Greece.

Pliny admired Lysippus for paying attention to the smallest details, such as hair.[78]

Pliny also said he did a huge statue of Zeus, sixty feet high, at Terentum, which was the largest statue in the ancient world except for the colossus of Rhodes. He also did a colossal statue of the Weary Heracles there, copies of which survive. When the Romans conquered Tarentum in 233 BC, the Zeus was too large for them to move, so instead they took the Heracles.[79]

Eros Stringing the Bow

Eros is, of course, the Greek equivalent of Cupid, who makes people fall in love by shooting arrows at them. The Greeks usually thought of Eros as young man, but Lysippus' Eros is an early adolescent who is not quite full-grown.

Lysippus' original statue was bronze, and the illustration shows a second century Roman copy in marble.

Once again, the delicate figure in a sinuous posture is a strong contrast with the muscular figures of the first generation of classical artists.

Oil Pourer

This statue shows an athlete pouring oil from a flask in his raised right arm into his left hand so he can apply it to his body (though both the arm and hand are lost). It is attributed to Lysippus or his circle. Because they trained and competed naked, Greek athletes used to coat their bodies with olive oil to protect themselves from the sun—and probably also to make their muscles shine in the sun to attract attention to themselves.

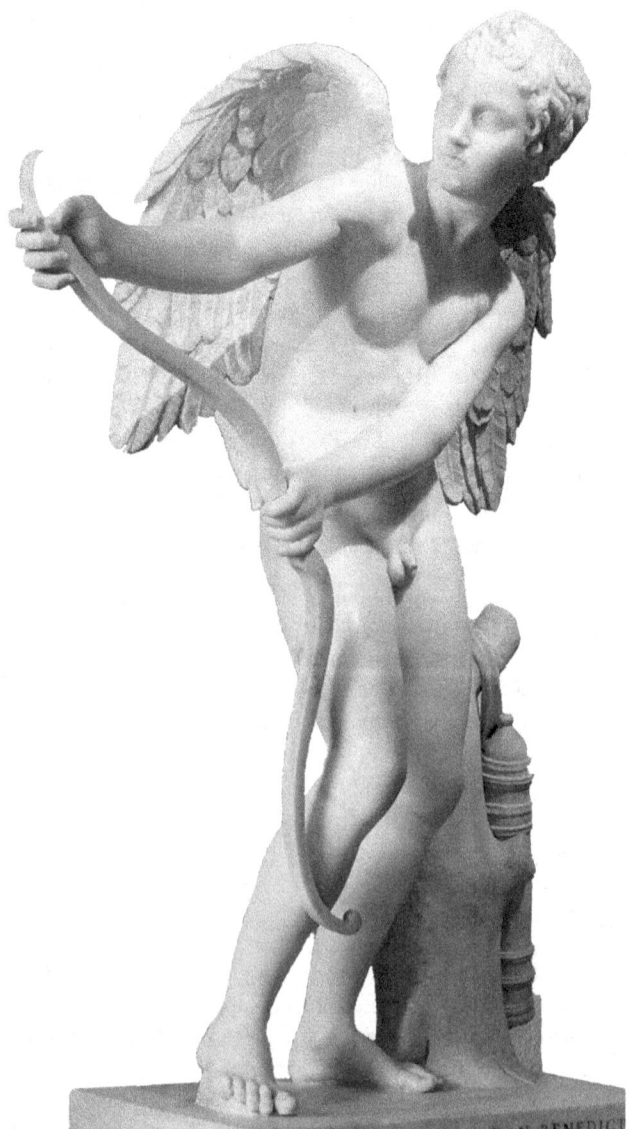

Figure 14-1: Roman Copy of Eros Stringing His Bow, Capitoline Museum
??british museum version may show up better but is lower resolution

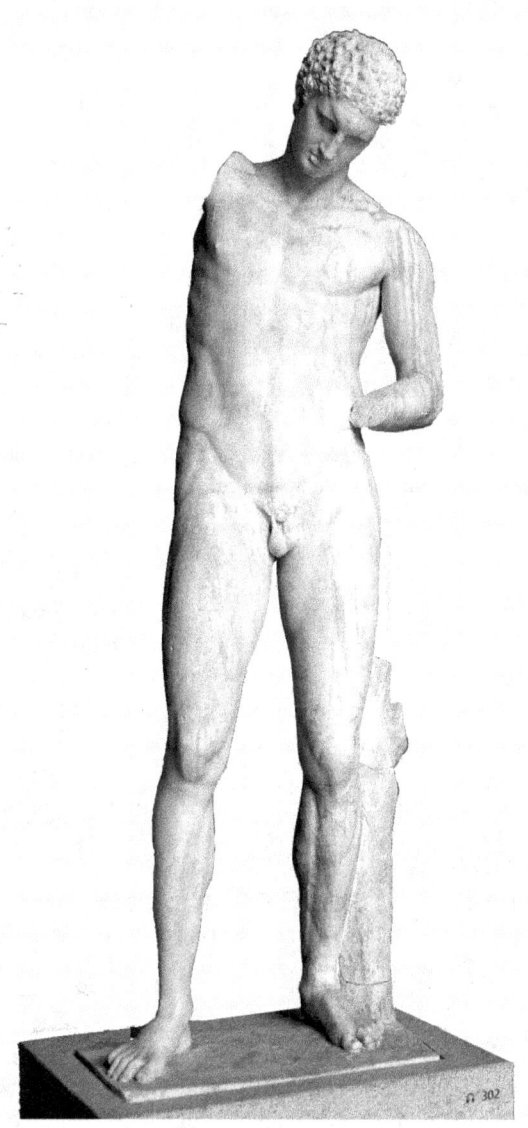

**Figure 14-2: Roman Copy of Oil Pourer,
Glyptothek Museum, Munich, Germany.**

The thin body of this statue is typical of Lysippus, following his canon. The more sinuous posture is also common in the works of Lysippus. Both of these features are similar to typical features of Praxiteles work.

Lysippus' original statue was bronze. Unfortunately, this marble copy in Munich was treated with acid in the nineteenth century to clean it, which removed a small layer from its surface. There is another marble copy in Dresden, but more of it is missing.

Apoxyomenos (Scraper)

The oil that athletes applied to their bodies attracted dust while they were training or competing. The Apoxyomenos—an athlete scraping the oil and dust off of his body—was a common subject of classical sculpture.

Lysippus' Apoxyomenos was his most renowned sculpture in ancient times. Pliny tells us that the general Marcus Vipsanius Agrippa installed it in the Baths of Agrippa in Rome, which he built in about 20 BC, that the Emperor Tiberius loved it so much that he moved it to his bedroom, and that a crowd in a theater responded to this move by shouting that the emperor should give them back the Apoxyomenos, shaming him into putting the statue back in the baths.[80]

A marble copy of Lysippus' original bronze was found in 1849 by archeologists digging in the Trastevere neighborhood of Rome.

It is a poised heroic figure of a man standing in contrapposto position, like many others, but with a bit of action added, as the athlete holds out one arm and uses the other to scrape it.

This statue is an excellent example of Lysippus' canon of ideal proportions, with a thinner figure and smaller head than the works of the first generation.

Hermes of Atalante

Hermes, whom the Romans called Mercury, was the messenger god and also the god of commerce and of trickery and theft. But the statue does not depict any specifics of the character of the god.

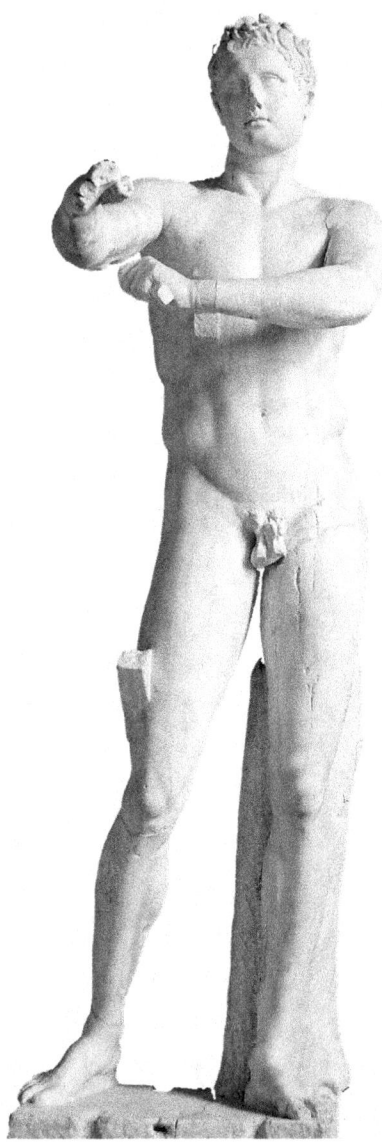

Figure 14-3: Roman Copy of the Apoxyomenos,
Vatican Museum

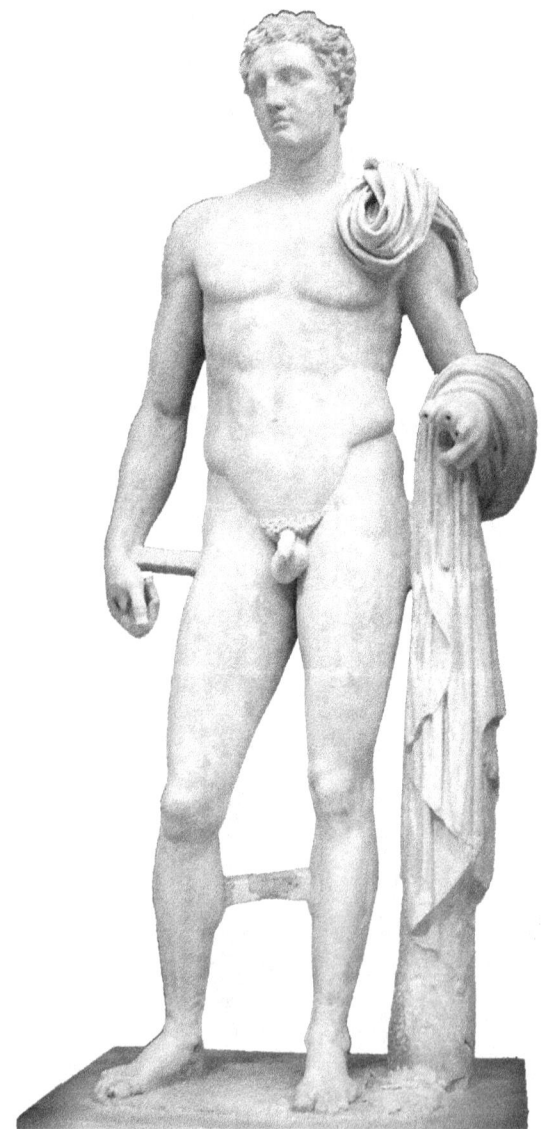

**Figure 14-3: Roman Copy of Hermes of Atalante,
National Archaeological Museum, Athens**

It is a poised, heroic statue of a man standing in contrapposto position, like many others.

It is not as thin as Lysippus' other statues, perhaps because the copy is not exact or perhaps because it was an early work. It is either by Lysippus or by one of his pupils. Like other statues we have seen, the original was bronze, but the surviving copy is marble.

Herakles Epitrapezios (Weary Heracles)

Lysippus created a bronze statue of the Weary Heracles (Herakles) which was melted down by crusaders in 1205, when they sacked Constantinople. This became one of the most admired statues of antiquity, and many copies were made. As we have seen, the original was a colossal statue in Tarentum.

The most famous copy is a marble statue made in the third century, signed by the otherwise unknown artist Glykon, and placed in the Baths of Caracalla. This statue was rediscovered in 1546 and was soon acquired by Cardinal Alessandro Farnese, grandson of Pope Paul II, which is why it is usually called the Farnese Hercules. This copy distorted Lysippus' original slightly to appeal to the third-century taste for heavy musculature.

Other copies have thinner hips and chest than the Farnese Hercules, but they are all too bulky to conform to Lysippus' canon. In fact, it is hard to imagine a statue of Hercules that would conform to his canon.

Though he is not thin, Heracles is tired out. The image of him resting, leaning on his club with his eyes downcast, contrasts with conventional idea of a fierce, active Hercules.

Alexander the Great

Lysippus was the personal sculptor of Alexander the Great, who was king from 336 BC until his death in 323 BC. Plutarch said that Alexander would not allow any other artist to make sculptures of him,[81] though this may be an exaggeration.

Lysippus probably made this bronze statue of Alexander

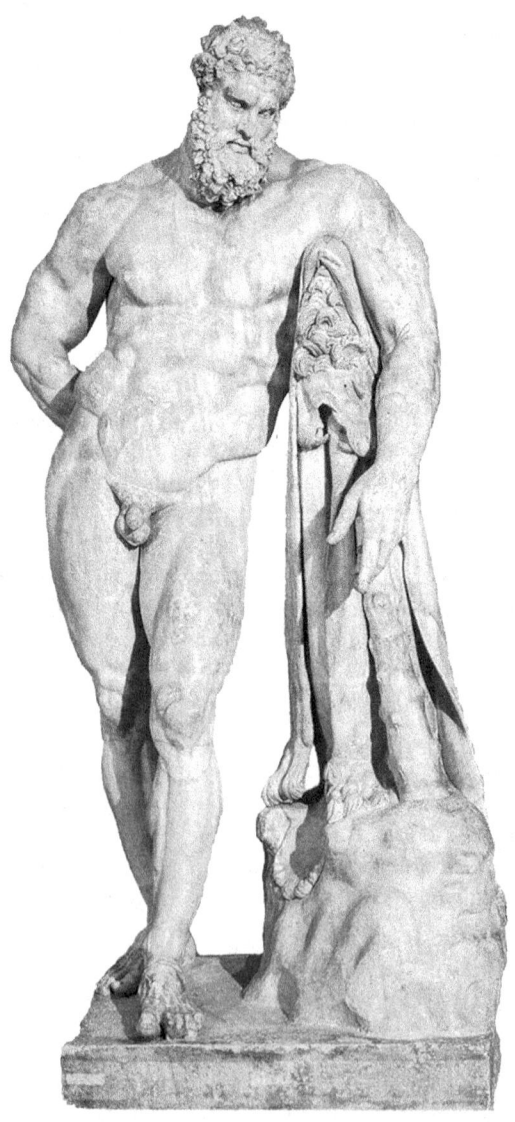

**Figure 14-5: Farnese Hercules, Copying Weary Heracles,
Museo Archeologico Nazionale, Naples**

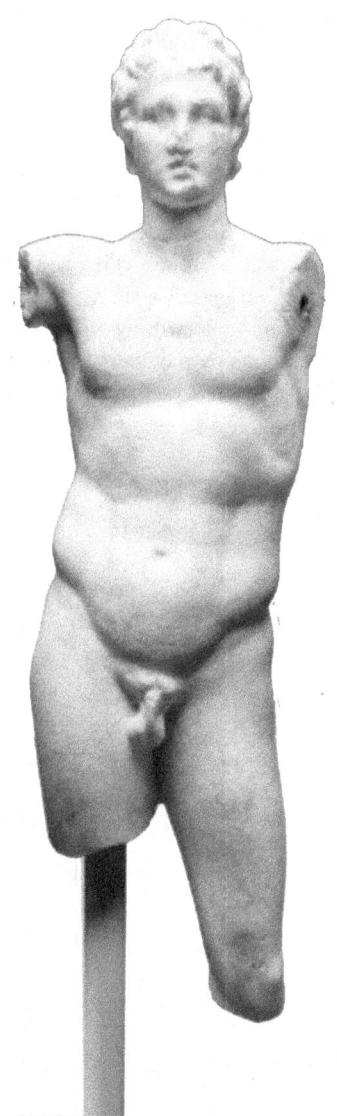

Figure 14-6: Small Roman Copy of Lysippus' Alexander the Great,
Getty Museum.

shortly before Alexander's death in 323 BC. In this statue, Alexander is naked and standing in the contrapposto position, like the heroic statues by Polyclitus and other artists of the first classical generation. But the statue is thinner than the statues of Polyclitus, another example showing that Lysippus' canon of proportions differed from his predecessor's.

Our illustration shows a Roman copy of the statue in marble, but we may also have an original bronze by Lysippus or his followers. In 2010, two men were arrested in Thessaloniki, Greece, for trying to sell a bronze version of this statue, which they apparently smuggled into Greece from Turkey, for 7 million Euros. Experts are trying to determine whether it is an original by Lysippus or a replica made by members of his studio.

Chapter 15
Leochares

Though Praxiteles, Scopas, and Lysippus are the three artists whom the ancients considered the greatest of their time, their contemporary Leochares created what is now the most famous sculpture of their time, the Apollo Belvedere, which some nineteenth century critics considered the greatest of all ancient sculptures.

In ancient times, Leochares' most renowned work was the statue of Zeus and Ganymede. His most famous portrait statues were chryselephantine statues of King Philip II of Macedon and his family members that were commissioned by King Philip to commemorate a victory over a coalition of Greek city states that paved the way for him to conquer all of Greece, statues installed in the Philippeion, which Phillip built as a monument to himself.

Leochares was an Athenian and was a member of the second Attic school, like Praxiteles and Scopas. Pliny dates him to the 102 Olympiad, 372-368 BC. There are a few other indications of his date. He worked on the Mausoleum at Halicarnassus, where in the sculptural reliefs on the four sides of the building were created by four Greek sculptors: Leochares, Bryaxis, Scopas, and Timotheus, and work there began in 352 BC. And his portrait statues of Macedonian royalty were commissioned after the Battle of Chaeronia in 338 BC.

Like Lysippus' statue of Alexander, the monument to Phillip's victory obviously brings us close to the end of the classical period and the beginning of the Hellenistic period.

Artemis Goddess of the Hunt

We have a Roman copy in marble produced in the second century AD of a bronze by Leochares showing the goddess

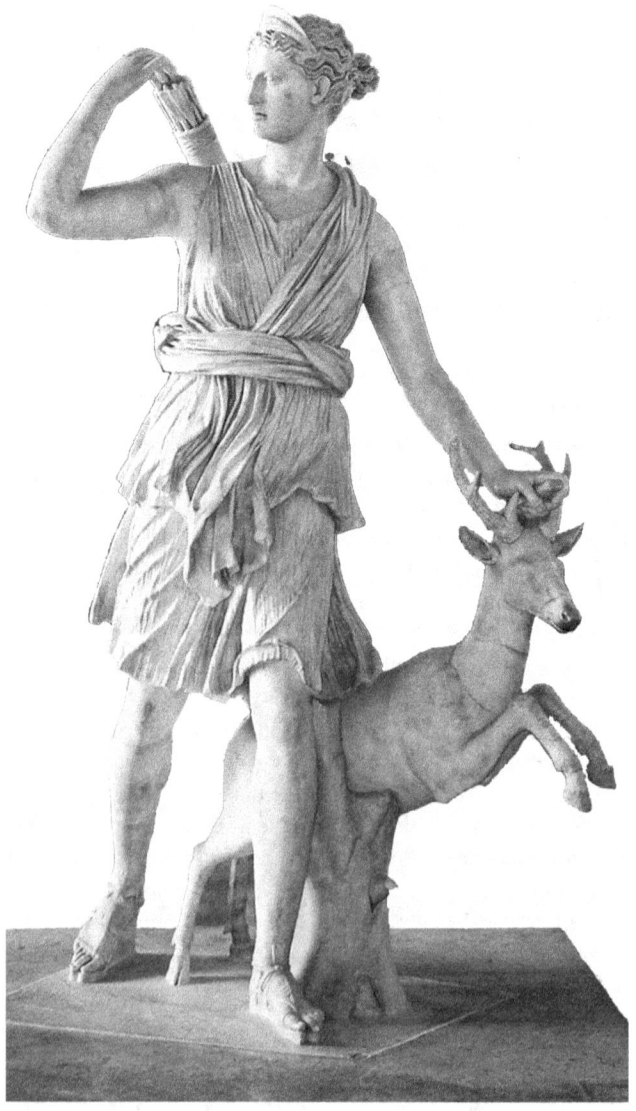

Figure 15-1: Diana of Versailles, Roman Copy of Artemis Goddess of the Hunt,
Louvre Museum

Artemis (whom the Romans called Diana) reaching over her shoulder with her right hand to remove an arrow from her quiver. There is a small cylindrical fragment in her left hand that was presumably part of a bow. The deer was added later, when the Roman statue was restored; it does not really make sense for a deer to accompany a hunter.

The drapery is very skillfully done. You can practically see it blowing in the wind. The face is very expressive: it seems serious and determined, but with the emotional restraint that the Greeks admired. The figure is captured in the midst of action, stepping forward as she prepares to shoot.

No one knows where the statue was initially located. It was discovered in Italy. It was moved to France in 1556, when Pope Paul IV gave it to King Henry II who put it in the Château de Fontainebleau. Henry IV put it in a specially designed gallery in the Palais du Louvre. Louis XIV moved it to Versailles. The French revolutionaries moved it back to the Louvre, where it remains today. But it kept the name that it got in Louis XIV time, so this Roman copy is still called Diana of Versailles.

It was restored by Barthélemy Prieur in 1602 and again by Bernard Lange in 1802.

Apollo Belvedere

We have a Roman copy made in the second century AD of Leochares bronze statue that came to be called Apollo Belvedere. But it is not an exact copy: Apollo is wearing Roman footwear, and there is no knowing whether the copyist changed other details.

Apollo is shown as an archer who has just shot an arrow. His left arm is still in the position where it would be to hold a bow while shooting, and a small fragment in the left hand shows that he was originally holding a bow. The face is very expressive and makes an interesting contrast with Leochares' Artemis: Apollo's face shows the same concentration as Artemis, but rather than determination before the act of shooting, it shows relaxation after shooting. The drapery and the curled hair are very skillfully done; the drapery seems more static than in the Artemis, but this may be in issue with the copy rather than the original.

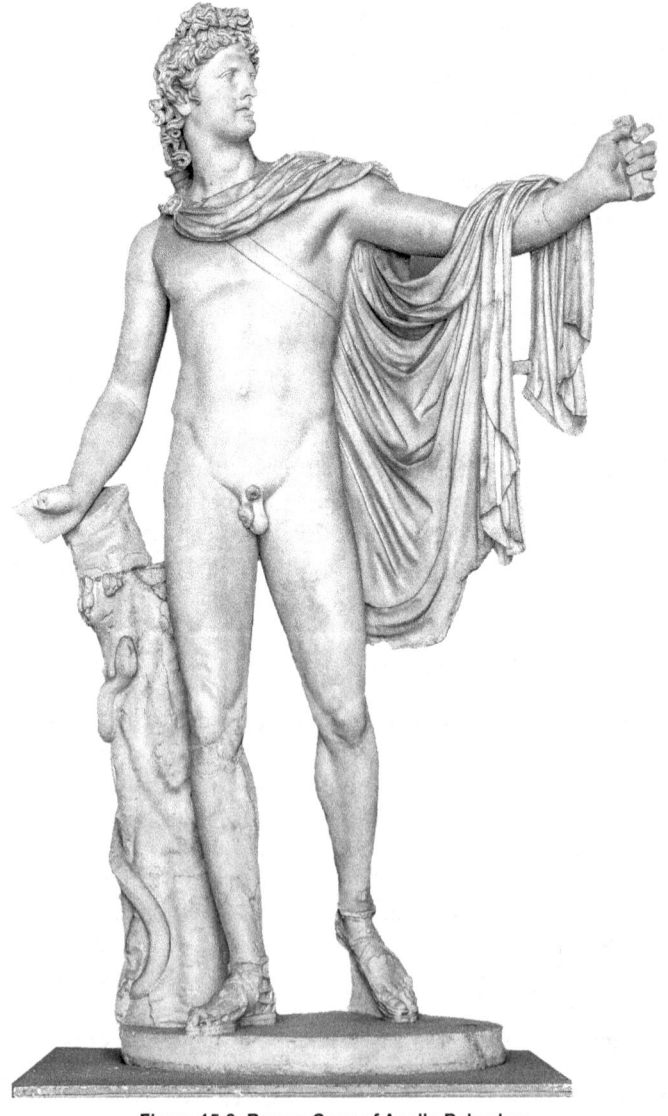

**Figure 15-2: Roman Copy of Apollo Belvedere,
Vatican Museum.**

Apollo very clearly has the thinner physique that was common in the age of Praxiteles rather than the more muscular physique of the age of Phidias.

This statue was discovered toward the end of the 1400s. In the first decade of the 1500s, it was moved to the Cortile delle Statue of the Vatican's Belvedere palace, which accounts for its name, and it became famous among artists, who made many sketches and copies of it. It became one of the most renowned ancient art works in the Eighteenth Century, after the German art historian Winckelmann said in 1755 that is was the best example of the "noble simplicity and quiet grandeur" (*edle Einfalt und stille Größe*) that he considered the essence of the classical ideal. Its reputation has declined since, but it remains clear that it is a great work of art.

Ganymede and the Eagle

The statue of Ganymede and the Eagle was Leochares' most admired work in ancient times. The original was bronze, but we have a Roman copy in marble.

According to the myth, Ganymede was the most beautiful youth in the world, so Zeus either sent an eagle or became an eagle himself to go down and bring him up to Olympus to be Zeus' cupbearer and lover. The myth goes back at least as far as Homer, who called him "godlike Ganymedes that was born the fairest of mortal men; wherefore the gods caught him up on high to be cupbearer to Zeus by reason of his beauty, that he might dwell with the immortals."[82]

In Leochares' statue, Ganymede has the usual thin build that was idealized during the age of Praxiteles, but he seems to have wider hips than most, making his form seem a bit more female.

This statue has a complex, dynamic composition that anticipates Hellenistic sculpture. Some have speculated that it is Hellenistic, but Pliny dates Leochares to the 102 Olympiad, 372-368 BC, and historians generally say that the Hellenistic period began when Alexander died in 323 BC, at least 45 years later, so it is likely that this work was produced toward the end of the classical period, late in Leochares' career, rather than in the Hellenistic period.

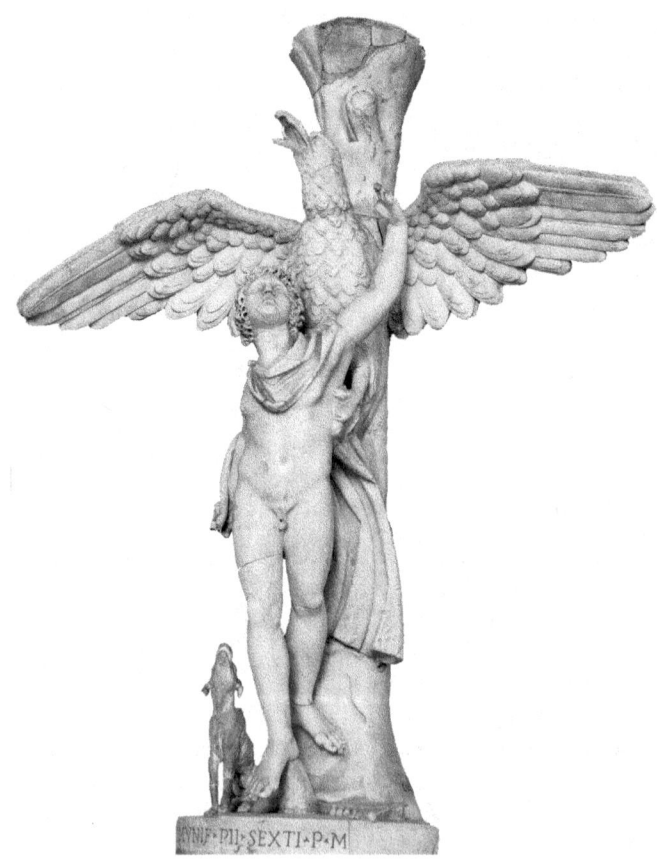

Figure 15-3: Roman copy of Ganymede and the Eagle, Vatican Museum

Part 5
Conclusion

Chapter 16
History and Art

Now that we have looked at the art works, it should be clear that the change in artistic style between the age of Phidias and the age of Praxiteles reflects the history of classical Greece.

The art of the age of Phidias expresses the spirit of the strong, self-confident Greek cities that won the Persian War. It features men with massive, powerful bodies, whose proportions were formalized in the Canon of Polyclitus, and it features fighting scenes. Phidias' metopes of the Parthenon, where the Lapiths fight and ultimately defeat the larger Centaurs, are a good symbol of the Greek city-states who defeated the larger Persian Empire.

The art of the age of Praxiteles expresses the spirit of the weakened Greek city states after the Peloponnesian War. Male statues generally have thinner, less muscular bodies, whose proportions were formalized in the Canon of Lysippus. The Weary Hercules has a more massive body, but he is tired and leaning on his club to rest, rather than fighting—a good symbol of the Greek city-states who were exhausted after the Peloponnesian War.

Two Ideals

The change in art also reflects a change from a moral ideal to an esthetic ideal.

The art of the age of Phidias is based on the moral ideal of what the Greeks called *arete*, which is often translated as virtue but which actually means something more like excellence—including virtue and other forms of excellence, such as athletic or intellectual accomplishment.

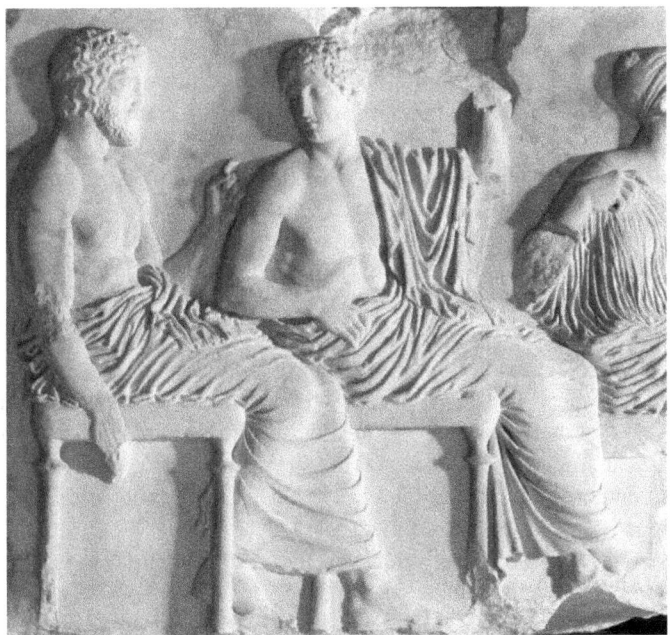

**Figure 16-1: Poseidon and Apollo from the Parthenon Frieze,
British Museum**

The muscular bodies show physical excellence.

The restrained emotions on the faces show the virtue that Greeks called *sophrosyne*, self-control or temperance. The one exception is Marsyas the satyr, who is carried away by his passions, and satyrs are comic characters who are looked down on.

Sometimes we also see other virtues. For example, the depiction of Poseidon and Apollo on the Parthenon Frieze is a good illustration of the cardinal virtue of wisdom, as the older god apparently gives wise advice to the younger.

The art of the age of Praxiteles is based on an esthetic ideal. Rather than inspiring people to achieve *arete*, it gives people an opportunity to escape from the hard realities of the time into a world of ideal beauty.

Often, there is a sexual element to that beauty. Most of us today can see it immediately in the female figures with "wet drapery" and in the nude Aphrodite of Cnidus, if we remember that women were excluded from public life in Athens and the artists were appealing to a male audience. But most of us today are a bit slower to see that, for most men in ancient Greece, the sexual appeal was also there in the statues of nude adolescents. Greek homosexuality was very different from homosexuality in our time: most men were bisexual and were attracted to adolescent youths as well as to women. We have seen that the great god Zeus himself, who was known for impregnating one mortal woman after another, also abducted the adolescent youth Ganymede, the most beautiful of mortals.

Whether it is the sensual appeal of women or of adolescents, these statues give their viewers an opportunity to escape into a world of beauty. Their sinuous posture adds to their sensual appeal. Today, we tend to make a sharp distinction between fine art and erotic art, but to the ancient Greeks, the erotic appeal was apparently part of the beauty of these works.

The age of Phidias celebrated the ideal of *arete*. The age of Praxiteles celebrated the ideal of beauty.

Lessons for our Time

Classical art is called "naturalistic" rather than "realistic." Its great advance over the primitive Kouros statues is its ability to represent people as they exist in nature, but it represents a humanistic ideal rather than representing people as they really are. For example, it is obviously not realistic to think that the Lapiths would be naked while they were fighting the Centaurs, but the nudity allows a representation of their ideal bodies as they are in nature. More generally, classical art represents ideally excellent and beautiful people as they would be in nature, but it does not represent less than ideal people as they would be in nature. We have only seen a couple of exceptions: the facial expression of the comic satyr Marsyas, and the self-portrait of Phidias, where his face looks old though he has an idealized, muscular body.

In the Hellenistic period, realism became more common, depicting people as they actually are, with all their flaws. For example, Lucian tells us that Demetrius of Alopece did a portrait sculpture of the Corinthian general Pellichus that was "bald, pot-bellied, half-naked; beard partly caught by the wind; protruding veins," and he contrasted this work with the idealizing sculpture of Cresilas.[83]

Today's art is very diverse, ranging from realism to abstraction to conceptual art, but one thing that our mainstream art lacks is the idealized naturalism of the classical Greeks. Perhaps today's artists could learn something by looking at the examples that we still have of these classical artworks, which inspired western artists for millennia. And perhaps we could all learn something by thinking about their ideals of *arete* and beauty.

End Matter

Appendix
How Did Phidias Die?

There are two accounts of Phidias' death. Plutarch tells us that he died in prison in Athens just before the Peloponnesian War began in 431 BC. Another source, purportedly quoting the historian Philochorus, says that he was exiled from Athens at this time, then built the Olympian Zeus in Elis, and then was executed by the Eleans after completing the Olympian Zeus.

Aristophanes, who is our most reliable source because he was a contemporary, says that Phidias was exiled shortly before the Peloponnesian War. He might have been imprisoned after being sentenced and died in prison before actually going into exile, confirming Plutarch's version of his death; or he might have gone into exile, gone to Elea, and built the Olympian Zeus, as the sources quoting Philochorus say. Neither of these sources is as reliable as Aristophanes. Plutarch wrote about 500 years later, which is plenty of time for legends to develop. Philochorus wrote about 150 years later, also enough time for legends to develop, and those quoting him do not seem reliable.

The sequence of Phidias' works changes depending on which account of his death we accept, and the date of the Olympian Zeus changes dramatically, since he might have done it before he began working on the Parthenon or after working on the Parthenon and being exiled. Because scholars are divided on the issue, there are wildly different estimates about the dates of the Olympian Zeus. For example, the Olympian Zeus is mentioned in three articles in Wikipedia: one says it was completed in 457 BC, one says 448 BC, and one says 435 BC.[84] But even the latest of these dates does not take into account that, if it were done after Phidias' exile, it would have been completed after the Peloponnesian War began in 431 BC, since all the sources say or imply that Phidias was sentenced to exile shortly before the war began.

It is obviously better to admit and explain the uncertainty, rather than providing these speculative dates as if they were known. We will look at the actual accounts of his exile and death that survive to see which is most plausible. Aristophanes' account is reliable but is cryptic. Plutarch and the quotes from Philochorus both present difficulties.

Aristophanes

Aristophanes is our most knowledgeable source, since he was a contemporary of the event, but he was a comic poet who often dealt in exaggerations and who made his points in ways that would fit into the rapid pace of comic drama. In his play "Peace" (421 BC). the god Hermes says:

HERMES Wise husbandmen, hearken to my words, if you want to know why she [Peace] was lost to you. The start of our misfortunes was the exile of Phidias; Pericles feared he might share his ill-luck, he mistrusted your peevish nature and, to prevent all danger to himself, he threw out that little spark, the Megarian decree, set the city aflame, and blew up the conflagration with a hurricane of war, so that the smoke drew tears from all Greeks both here and over there. At the very outset of this fire our vines were a-crackle, our casks knocked together; it was beyond the power of any man to stop the disaster, and Peace disappeared.[85]

This quotation from Aristophanes is compatible with either account of Phidias' death. At the time, imprisonment was not a punishment for crimes. The available punishments were fines, exile, or death, and a prisoner was just jailed temporarily before being punished, as Socrates was jailed temporarily before being executed. Thus, Phidias might have been sentenced to being exiled, been put in jail temporarily before leaving Athens, and died in jail, as Plutarch says. Or he might have actually gone into exile, completed the Olympian Zeus, and then died, as the other source says. Aristophanes skips over the details and states it in a very abbreviated way, because the contemporary audience would have known what happened without being told.

Plutarch

Plutarch's account mentions the Megarian decree before it mentions Phidias death. We will have to quote at length to compare his account with Aristophanes statement that Pericles promulgated the Megarian decree shortly after Phidias' death:

the Megarians … brought their complaint that from every market-place and from all the harbours over which the Athenians had control, they were excluded and driven away, contrary to the common law and the formal oaths of the Greeks; ….

… it does not seem probable that the war would have come upon the Athenians for any remaining reasons, if only they could have been persuaded to rescind their decree against the Megarians and be reconciled with them. And therefore, since it was Pericles who was most of all opposed to this, and who incited the people to abide by their contention with the Megarians, he alone was held responsible for the war.

They say that when an embassy had come from Lacedaemon to Athens to treat of these matters, and Pericles was shielding himself behind the plea that a certain law prevented his taking down the tablet on which the decree was inscribed, Polyalces, one of the ambassadors, cried: "Well then, don't take it down, but turn the tablet to the wall; surely there's no law preventing that." Clever as the proposal was, however, not one whit the more did Pericles give in. He must have secretly cherished, then, as it seems, some private grudge against the Megarians; but by way of public and open charge he accused them of appropriating to their own profane uses the sacred territory of Eleusis, and proposed a decree that a herald be sent to them, the same to go also to the Lacedaemonians with a denunciation of the Megarians. This decree, at any rate, is the work of Pericles, and aims at a reasonable and humane justification of his course. But after the herald who was sent, Anthemocritus, had been put to death through the agency of the Megarians, as it was believed, Charinus proposed a decree against them, to the effect that there be irreconcilable and implacable enmity on the part of Athens towards them, and that whosoever of the Megarians should set foot on the soil of Attica be punished with death; and that the generals, whenever they should take their ancestral oath of office, add to their oath this clause, that they would invade the Megarid twice during each succeeding year; and that Anthemocritus be buried honourably at the Thriasian gates, which are now called the Dipylum.

Well, then, whatever the original ground for enacting the decree,—and it is no easy matter to determine this,—the fact that it was not rescinded all men alike lay to the charge of Pericles. Only, some say that he persisted in his refusal in a lofty spirit and with a clear perception of the best interests of the city, regarding the injunction laid upon it as a test of its submissiveness, and its compliance as a confession of weakness; while others hold that it was rather with a sort of arrogance and love of strife, as well as for the display of his power, that he scornfully defied the Lacedaemonians.

But the worst charge of all, and yet the one which has the most vouchers, runs something like this. Phidias the sculptor was contractor for the great statue [of Athena Parthenos], as I have said, and being admitted to the friendship of Pericles, and acquiring the greatest influence with him, made some enemies through the jealousy which he excited; others also made use of him to test the people and see what sort of a judge it would be in a case where Pericles was involved. These latter persuaded one Menon, an assistant of Phidias, to take a suppliant's seat in the market-place and demand immunity for punishment in case he should bring information and accusation against Phidias. The people accepted the man's proposal, and formal prosecution of Phidias was made in the assembly. Embezzlement, indeed, was not proven, for the gold of the statue, from the very start, had been so wrought upon and cast about it by Phidias, at the wise suggestion of Pericles, that it could all be taken off and weighed, and this is what Pericles actually ordered the accusers of Phidias to do at this time.

But the reputation of his works nevertheless brought a burden of jealous hatred upon Phidias, and especially the fact that when he wrought the battle of the Amazons on the shield of the goddess, he carved out a figure that suggested himself as a bald old man lifting on high a stone with both hands, and also inserted a very fine likeness of Pericles fighting with an Amazon. And the attitude of the hand, which holds out a spear in front of the face of Pericles, is cunningly contrived as it were with a desire to conceal the resemblance, which is, however, plain to be seen from either side. Phidias, accordingly, was led away to prison, and died there of sickness; but some say of poison which the enemies of Pericles provided, that they might bring calumny upon him. And to Menon the informer, on motion of Glycon, the people gave immunity from taxation, and enjoined upon the generals to make provision for the man's safety.[86]

This passage uses "the Megarian decree" to refer to three separate decrees:

The first was an economic embargo: "that from every market-place and from all the harbours over which the Athenians had control, they were excluded and driven away."

The second was sending a herald to denounce them: "[Pericles] proposed a decree that a herald be sent to them, the same to go also to the Lacedaemonians with a denunciation of the Megarians. This decree, at any rate, is the work of Pericles...."

The third was proposed after the killing of the herald, which was considered a sacrilege at the time, and this third decree was tantamount to a declaration of war: "Charinus proposed a decree against them, to the effect that there be irreconcilable and implacable enmity on the part of Athens towards them, and that whosoever of the Megarians should set foot on the soil of Attica be punished with death; and that the generals, whenever they should take their ancestral oath of office, add to their oath this clause, that they would invade the Megarid twice during each succeeding year." Charinus proposed this, but Pericles often had others make the proposals that he supported.

The earliest of these decrees, the economic boycott, was adopted in 334-333 BC. But Aristophanes is clearly referring to a decree that led very quickly to the Peloponnesian War, which began in 331 BC, so he must be talking about one of the two later decrees.

Plutarch talks about these decrees and the charges that people made against Pericles because of them before he talks about the charges of theft and blasphemy against Phidias. But he does not say that this is the sequence in which they happened, and he does not say when the third decree was adopted, just that it was proposed. Thus, it is possible to reconcile this account with Aristophanes by saying that, after Phidias was convicted of blasphemy, Pericles pushed for the adoption of this third decree, which was virtually a declaration of war and led immediately to the Peloponnesian War.[87]

The weak point of Plutarch's account, however, is that Thucydides, the contemporary historian who is the best source of information about the Peloponnesian War, mentions only the first decree, does not mention sending a herald to Sparta who was killed, and does not mention Charinus or his decree. Thucydides talks only about the Megarian decree that was an economic boycott: he says that the Spartans sent a herald to Athens in 432-431 who said that there would be peace if Athens revoked the economic boycott, that Pericles gave a speech to the Athenians saying they should not revoke the decree because they could win the war, and that Pericles' speech convinced the Athenians and caused the war.[88]

Since Thucydides, as a contemporary and a careful historian, is a more reliable source than Plutarch, it seems most likely that Aristophanes was thinking about this speech refusing to revoke the Megarian decree when he said that Pericles adopted the Megarian decree to solidify his power after the conviction of Phidias, and that this act led quickly to war.

The Scholiasts

The source that says Phidias was exiled, built the Olympian Zeus in Elis, and was executed by the Eleans is purportedly the third-century BC historian Philochorus, as quoted in two scholia on Aristophanes' play *Peace*. A scholium is a note written in the margin of a manuscript, and these two scholia were found in a manuscript of Peace near the quotation from Aristophanes that we already looked at.

The first scholium says:

Under the year of the archonship of Pythodorus [432-431 BC], Philochorus says that 'the golden statue of Athena was set up in the great temple, having forty-four talents weight of gold, under the superintendence of Pericles and the workmanship of Phidias. And Phidias, appearing to have misappropriated ivory for the scales [of the dragon] was condemned. And having gone as an exile to Elis, he is said to have made the statue of Zeus at Olympia; but having finished this, he was put to death by the Elians under the archonship of Sythodorus, who is the seventh from this one [that is, the seventh archon after Pythodorus].'

The second scholium, further down in the margin of the manuscript, says:

Phidias, as Philochorus says in the archonship of Pythodorus, having made the statue of Athena, pilfered the gold from the dragons of the chryselephantine Athena, for which he was found guilty and sentenced to banishment; but having come to Elis, and having made among the Elians the statue of the Olympian Zeus, and having been found guilty by them of peculation, he was put to death.[89]

These two scholia do not seem very reliable. Both purport to quote Philochorus, but they contradict each other, with the first saying that Phidias was accused of stealing ivory and the second that he was accused of stealing gold. In addition, the first scholium makes an error by mentioning the archon Sythodorus, who is not mentioned elsewhere and who apparently did not exist, since the seventh archon after Pythodorus was actually Stratocles.

Both also get the date of the completion of Athena Parthenos wrong, since the statue was clearly completed before 432-431 BC, when Pythodorus was archon. Some scholars tried to deal with this problem by reading Theodorus instead of Pythodorus and Pythodorus instead of Sythodorus,[90] but that would mean that Phidias was tried in 438-437 BC, when Theodorus was archon, which contradicts Aristophanes' statement that he was tried shortly before the Peloponnesian War began in 431. We can get around this error by reading these scholia as saying that Phidias stole the gold or ivory during the archonship of Pythodorus, though he had completed the statue earlier. This would have been possible, since he was still working on the Parthenon ornamentation for many years after finishing Athena Parthenos, but it would still be an error to say the Athena Parthenos was set up when Pythodorus was archon.

The reliability of these scholia is definitely questionable because of the contradiction about whether gold or ivory was stolen, because of the error about when the Athena Parthenos was set up, and because one scholium uses the name of the non-existent archon Sythodorus.

Conclusion

We can see that both sources are not completely reliable. Plutarch gives an explanation of the Megarian decree that contradicts Thucydides and so is probably incorrect. The scholiasts make several blatant errors. The main lesson here is that so many of the ancient sources are unreliable that we cannot be certain about what actually happened.

But there is one other important point against the scholia: they say Phidias went into exile immediately before the Peloponnesian War and then built the Olympian Zeus, since they say he was exiled when Pythodorus was archon, and the war began during the final months of his term.[91] The Olympian Zeus was a tremendous project that required Phidias and his assistants to build a workshop in Olympia, that required a huge expenditure on ivory and gold, and that the scholia say took seven years (the terms of seven archons) to complete. It is not plausible that Elis would devote so many resources to building this statue at a time when it needed its resources for war.

Some scholars try to deal with this problem by saying that the trial and exile must have been earlier (for example, when Theodorus was archon), but there is no justification for this. All of the sources imply or say explicitly that the war came very soon after Phidias' trial. The scholia themselves say that Phidias was tried during the archonship of Pythodorus (432-431 BC), who was archon at the beginning of the Peloponnesian War, and that Phidias then went to Elis and began the Olympian Zeus—which implies that this expensive project was initiated and carried out during war time.

We can conclude that it is difficult to determine how Phidias died. Plutarch may be right to say that he died in jail in Athens. Or the scholiasts may be right to say that he went into exile and died later—and it is plausible that he would go into exile in Elis, since they would welcome him because of his earlier work on Olympian Zeus.

But we can also conclude with some confidence that the Olympian Zeus was an earlier work and was not created after Phidias was exiled. It is not plausible the he created it during the Peloponnesian War, after being exiled, as the scholiasts claim.

As we saw in Chapter 4, it is more plausible that he built it before Pericles moved the treasury of the Delian League to Athens in 454 BC that after that date he focused on rebuilding the Acropolis—and that he became the supervisor of all construction on the Acropolis precisely because he had earlier experience supervising the huge job of creating Olympian Zeus.

Licensing Information

All of the illustrations in this book are either in the public domain or licensed through Creative Commons Attribution/ShareAlike license. This section contains information required by this license, which is available at:
https://creativecommons.org/licenses/by-sa/4.0/

All illustrations except for the cover illustration have been modified by converting them from color to black and white and by adjusting brightness and color to make them clearer in black and white. All illustrations have been modified by removing the background. Thanks to the following photographers for sharing their work through the Creative Commons:

Figure 3-2: Peplos Kore. Photograph courtesy of Marsyas.

Figure 3-3: The Tyrannicides. Photograph courtesy of Miguel Hermoso Cuesta.

Figure 3-4: Ephebos (Boy). Photograph courtesy of Ricardo André Frantz.

Figure 4-1: Anacreon. Photograph courtesy of ChrisO.

Figure 4-8a: Image from the frieze of the Parthenon. Photograph courtesy of Urban.

Figure 4-10a: A Metope from the Parthenon. Photograph courtesy of Marie-Lan Nguyen.

Figure 4-11a: The East Pediment. Photograph courtesy of Tilemahos Efthimiadis.

Figure 4-11b: The West Pediment. Photograph courtesy of Tilemahos Efthimiadis.

Figure 4-12: Statue of Dionysus. Photograph courtesy of Marie-Lan Nguyen.

Figure 4-13: Statue of the Three Fates. Photograph courtesy of Carole Raddato.

Figure 5-1: The Diskobolos. Photograph courtesy of Livioandronico2013.

Figure 5-4: The Minotaur. Photograph courtesy of Carole Raddato.

Figure 5-5: Theseus. Photograph courtesy of Zde.

Figure 7-1: Wounded Amazon. Photograph courtesy of Marie-Lan Nguyen.

Figure 7-2: Athena of Velletri. Photograph courtesy of Kimberly Vardeman.

Figure 8-1: Roman Copy of Nemesis of Rhamnus. Photograph courtesy of Zde.

Figure 9-1: Roman copy of Nike. Photograph courtesy of Roccuz.

Figure 10-1: Nike Adjusting Her Sandal. Photograph courtesy of Marsyas.

Figure 10-2: Roman copy of Dancing Maenad. Photograph courtesy of Luis García.

Figure 12.2: Hermes and the Infant Dionysus. Photograph courtesy of Dwaisman.

Figure 12.5: Original Apollo Sauroktonos. Photograph courtesy of Wmpearl.

Figure 13-1: Head of Hygieia. Photograph courtesy of Marsyas.

Figure 13-2: Head of Meleager. Photograph courtesy of Marie-Lan Nguyen.

Figure 14-1: Eros Stringing His Bow. Photograph courtesy of Marie-Lan Nguyen.

Figure 14-2: Oil Pourer. Photograph courtesy of José Luiz Bernardes Ribeiro.

Figure 14-3: Hermes of Atalante. Photograph courtesy of Ricardo André Frantz.

Figure 15-1: Diana of Versailles. Photograph courtesy of Eric Gaba.

Figure 15-2: Apollo Belvedere, Roman Copy. Photograph courtesy of Belmonte.

Notes

1. Plutarch, *Parallel Lives*, translated by Bernadotte Perrin (Loeb Classical Library, 1916) Life of Pericles 2.1-2.

2. William Smith, editor, *Dictionary of Greek and Roman Biography and Mythology* (London, Tayler, Walton & Maberly, 1849) vol. 1, p. 393.

3. Plutarch, Life of Pericles 12.3.

4. Herodotus *Histories* 1.31. Herodotus tells us that, when Croesus asked Solon who were the happiest people he knew of, thinking that Solon would say that Croesus was happy because of his wealth, Solon told him the story of these brothers and said they were among the happiest he could think of.

5. The date is from the inscribed Parian Chronicle.

6. Smith, *Dictionary*, vol. 1, p. 393.

7. For example, Hodder Michael Westropp, *Handbook of Archaeology: Egyptian-Greek-Etruscan-Roman*, second edition (London, George Bell & Sons, 1878) says Myron and Polyclitus were earlier than Phidias.

8. Plutarch, Life of Pericles 31.4.

9. Plutarch, Life of Pericles 13.9.

10. Plutarch, Life of Pericles 31.2-5.

11. See appendix.

12. Pausanias, *Description of Greece*, translated by W.H.S. Jones and H.A. Ormerod, (Cambridge, MA, Harvard University Press; London, William Heinemann Ltd. 1918) 1.28.2.

13. Pausanias, *Description of Greece* 10.10.1-2.

14. Smith, *Dictionary*, vol. 3, p. 249.

15. Pliny the Elder. *The Natural History*. translated by John Bostock and H.T. Riley (London. Taylor and Francis, 1855) 34.19.

16. Pliny, *Natural History* 5.11.9.

17. Pausanias, *Description of Greece* 5.11.1. Here is the rest of his description from Pausanias 5.11.2-10:

> [2] The throne is adorned with gold and with jewels, to say nothing of ebony and ivory. Upon it are painted figures and wrought images. There are four Victories, represented as dancing women, one at each foot of the throne, and two others at the base of each foot. On each of the two front feet are set Theban children ravished by sphinxes, while under the sphinxes Apollo and Artemis are shooting down the children of Niobe.

> [3] Between the feet of the throne are four rods, each one stretching from foot to foot. The rod straight opposite the entrance has on it seven images; how the eighth of them disappeared nobody knows. These must be intended to be copies of obsolete contests, since in the time of Phidias contests for boys had not yet been introduced.1 The figure of one binding his own head with a ribbon is said to resemble in appearance Pantarces, a stripling of Elis said to have been the love of Phidias. Pantarces too won the wrestling-bout for boys at the eighty-sixth Festival.

> [4] On the other rods is the band that with Heracles fights against the Amazons. The number of figures in the two parties is twenty-nine, and Theseus too is ranged among the allies of Heracles. The throne is supported not only by the feet, but also by an equal number of pillars standing between the feet. It is impossible to go under the throne, in the way we enter the inner part of the throne at Amyclae. At Olympia there are screens constructed like walls which keep people out.

> [5] Of these screens the part opposite the doors is only

covered with dark-blue paint; the other parts show pictures by Panaenus. Among them is Atlas, supporting heaven and earth, by whose side stands Heracles ready to receive the load of Atlas, along with Theseus; Perithous, Hellas, and Salamis carrying in her hand the ornament made for the top of a ship's bows; then Heracles' exploit against the Nemean lion, the outrage committed by Ajax on Cassandra,

[6] Hippodameia the daughter of Oenomaus with her mother, and Prometheus still held by his chains, though Heracles has been raised up to him. For among the stories told about Heracles is one that he killed the eagle which tormented Prometheus in the Caucasus, and set free Prometheus himself from his chains. Last in the picture come Penthesileia giving up the ghost and Achilles supporting her; two Hesperides are carrying the apples, the keeping of which, legend says, had been entrusted to them. This Panaenus was a brother of Phidias; he also painted the picture of the battle of Marathon in the painted portico at Athens.

[7] On the uppermost parts of the throne Phidias has made, above the head of the image, three Graces on one side and three Seasons on the other. These in epic poetry2 are included among the daughters of Zeus. Homer too in the Iliad3 says that the Seasons have been entrusted with the sky, just like guards of a king's court. The footstool of Zeus, called by the Athenians thranion, has golden lions and, in relief, the fight of Theseus against the Amazons, the first brave deed of the Athenians against foreigners.

[8] On the pedestal supporting the throne and Zeus with all his adornments are works in gold: the Sun mounted on a chariot, Zeus and Hera, Hephaestus, and by his side Grace. Close to her comes Hermes, and close to Hermes Hestia. After Hestia is Eros receiving Aphrodite as she rises from the sea, and Aphrodite is being crowned by Persuasion. There are also reliefs of Apollo with Artemis, of Athena and of Heracles; and near the end of

the pedestal Amphitrite and Poseidon, while the Moon is driving what I think is a horse. Some have said that the steed of the goddess is a mule not a horse, and they tell a silly story about the mule.

[9] I know that the height and breadth of the Olympic Zeus have been measured and recorded; but I shall not praise those who made the measurements, for even their records fall far short of the impression made by a sight of the image. Nay, the god himself according to legend bore witness to the artistic skill of Phidias. For when the image was quite finished Phidias prayed the god to show by a sign whether the work was to his liking. Immediately, runs the legend, a thunderbolt fell on that part of the floor where down to the present day the bronze jar stood to cover the place.

[10] All the floor in front of the image is paved, not with white, but with black tiles. In a circle round the black stone runs a raised rim of Parian marble, to keep in the olive oil that is poured out. For olive oil is beneficial to the image at Olympia, and it is olive oil that keeps the ivory from being harmed by the marshiness of the Altis. On the Athenian Acropolis the ivory of the image they call the Maiden is benefited, not by olive oil, but by water. For the Acropolis, owing to its great height, is over-dry, so that the image, being made of ivory, needs water or dampness.

18. Pausanias, *Description of Greece* 6.25.1.

19. Pausanias, *Description of Greece* 6.26.3.

20. Pausanias, *Description of Greece* 9.4.1.

21. Pausanias, *Description of Greece* 9.4.2.

22. Quoted in "Athena Promachos," Bulletin of the Institute of Classical Studies. 56. 2013,

23. Pausanias, *Description of Greece* 9.4.2.

24. Plutarch, Life of Pericles 13.4.

25. Pausanias, *Description of Greece* 1.24.5,7.

26. Plato, *Hippias Major*, 290.

27. G. M. A. Richter, *Greek Art: A Handbook*, third edition, (London, Phaidon Press, 1963) p. 103.

28. Pliny, *Natural History* 34.19.

29. Pliny, *Natural History* 34.19.

30. Smith, *Dictionary*, vol. 2, p. 1130.

31. H. Edith Legge, A Short History of the Ancient Greek Sculptors (New York, James Pott & Co. and London T. Fisher Unwin, 1903) p. 73.

32. Galen, *De placitis Hippocratis et Platonis* (On the doctrines of Hippocrates and Plato) 5.3; noted in Richard Tobin, "The Canon of Polykleitos" American Journal of Archaeology 79.4 (October 1975:307–321) pp308f.

33. Claudius Aelianus (Aelian), *Varia Historia* (Various History), translated by Thomas Stanley, 1665. 14.8.

34. Pliny, *Natural History* 34.19.

35. Thucydides, *Peloponnesian War* 4.133.

36. Pausanias, *Description of Greece* 2.17.4.

37. Pliny, *Natural History* 34.19.

38. Pliny, *Natural History* 34.19.

39. Pausanias, *Description of Greece* I.25.1, I.28.2.

40. Plutarch, Life of Pericles 3.2.

41. Pausanias, *Description of Greece* 9.34.

42. Pliny, *Natural History* 36.4.

43. Pliny, *Natural History* 36.4, Pausanias, *Description of Greece* 9.34.

44. Pliny, *Natural History* 36.4.

45. Pausanias, *Description of Greece* 1.33.3.

46. Pausanias, *Description of Greece* 5.10.8.

47. Pausanias, *Description of Greece* 5.26.1.

48. Vitruvius, *De Architectura* 4.1.10.

49. Pausanias, *Description of Greece* 1.26.7.

50. Pliny, *Natural History* 34.19.

51. Pausanias, *Description of Greece* 1.26.7.

52. Plutarch, Life of Phocion 19.1.

53. Pliny, *Natural History* 34.19.

54. Pliny, *Natural History* 34.19.

55. Pausanias, *Description of Greece* 9.30.1.

56. Pausanias, *Description of Greece* 8.30.10.

57. Martin Robertson, *A Shorter History of Greek Art* (Cambridge University Press, 1981) p. 139.

58. Pausanias, *Description of Greece* 9.16.2.

59. Pliny, *Natural History* 34.19.

60. Pliny, *Natural History* 34.19.

61. Pausanias, *Description of Greece* 8.9.1.

62. Pseudo-Plutarch, *Lives of the Ten Orators* 9. Pliny, *Natural History* 34.19.

63. Adolf Furtwängler, *Meisterwerke der Griechischen Plastik* (Berlin, 1893).

64. Pausanias, *Description of Greece* 5.17.3.

65. Pliny, *Natural History* 36.4.

66. Pseudo-Lucian, *Affairs of the Heart* 13.

67. Pliny, *Natural History* 36.4. This story originated with the historian Posidippus and was retold by Pseudo-Lucian, Valerius Maximus, and Athenæus, as well as by Pliny.

68. Pliny, *Natural History* 34.8.

69. Pausanias, *Description of Greece* 1.20.1-2.

70. Pausanias, *Description of Greece* 8.45.5-7.

71. Pausanias, *Description of Greece* 8.45.6.

72. Callistratus, *Descriptions of Statues* 2.1-4 cited in Andrew Stewart, *One Hundred Greek Sculptors: Their Careers and Extant Works*, New Perseus Monographs, http://perseus.uchicago.edu/cgi-bin/philologic/getobject.pl?c.2:2:4:1. NewPerseusMonographs

73. Pausanias, *Description of Greece* 1.43.6.

74. Pliny, *Natural History* 33.19.

75. Pliny, *Natural History* 34.17.

76. Pliny, *Natural History* 34.19.

77. Cicero, *Brutus* also known as *Of Famous Orators*, 296.

78. Pliny, *Natural History* 34.19.

79. Pliny, *Natural History* 34.18.

80. Pliny, *Natural History* 34.19.

81. Plutarch, Life of Alexander, 4.1.

82. Homer, *Iliad*, translated by A.T. Murray (Cambridge, MA., Harvard University Press; London, William Heinemann, 1924) Book 20, lines 233-235.

83. Lucian of Samosata, *The Lover of Lies* (*Philopseudes*), translated as *The Liar* by H. W. Fowler and F. G. Fowler (Oxford University Press, 1905) 18-20.

84. The statue was completed in 457 BC according to https://en.wikipedia.org/wiki/Temple_of_Zeus,_Olympia, in 448 BC according to https://en.wikipedia.org/wiki/List_of_Ancient_Greek_temples, and in 435 BC according to https://en.wikipedia.org/wiki/Statue_of_Zeus_at_Olympia. All of these are based on sources that gave the date as if they knew it with some certainty.

85. Aristophanes, *Peace*, anonymous translation for the Athenian Society, London, 1912.

86. Plutarch, Life of Pericles 30.4-31.5.

87. This approach to reconciling the two accounts was suggested

by James McDonald, "Supplementing Thucydides' Account Of The Megarian Decree," ElAnt, Vol. 2, Number 3, October 1994.

88. Thucydides, *The Peloponnesian War*, 1.139-1.145.

89. Smith, *Dictionary*, vol. 3, p. 247.

90. Smith, *Dictionary*, vol. 3, p. 247.

91. Thucydides, *Peloponnesian War* 2.2.

www.ingramcontent.com/pod-product-compliance
Lightning Source LLC
Chambersburg PA
CBHW071314220526
45468CB00001B/371